SPEAKING OF THE DEAD

Written by: Chelsea L. Tolman

Speaking of the dead by Chelsea L. Tolman

ISBN: 978-1-7329484-0-2 (ebook)
ISBN: 978-1-7329484-1-9 (paperback)

Contributors:
Forward written by Robert J. Labrum
Photography by Tyson J. Rider

Speaking of the dead by Chelsea L. Tolman

So many words to say, so many people to thank. Jamie Duncan Kennedy, you have been my cheering squad for more years than I am willing to admit (only because it shows our age) and you said it first, that I would be a published author one day, I should have listened to you then. Rob Labrum, my husband, my other half and champion, thank you for the hours of reading and editing, for loving me unconditionally, encouraging me to hit the send button and for bringing Kye into my life, I couldn't have asked for a more beautiful step-son. Judy Tolman, my mother, thank you for the hours of talking with me on the phone before, during and after as these stories happened in real life and for loving and encouraging what I chose as a career. Sam Tolman, my father, thank you for shining like the sun and sharing that loving and unconditional light with all of your children. Brian, Ron, Amity, Jason and Braden, my siblings, thank you for loving my weirdness, accepting my faults and forgiving my inability to remember birthdays, even when its on the calendar, in red, every year.

Speaking of the dead by Chelsea L. Tolman

FOREWORD

Morticians and funeral directors have a place in our popular culture, but unfortunately, it's usually as oddballs and weirdos. The characters in Six Feet Under were absurdly dramatized to draw in ratings. There was Dan Akroyd's role in My Girl – a dismissive father who cared more for the dead than his own daughter. Don't get me started on Jack Black's unsettling portrayal in Bernie. The point is, we never see morticians as normal people with normal lives, because they handle dead bodies, drain their blood, and – eew! Right?

Before I met Chelsea Tolman, the only other mortician I had encountered was a grim-faced man who led me silently to the bare room where my dead father lay on a cold, bare metal table, covered by a nondescript white sheet. The room was sterile, and my father was pale, misshapen, and looked like he would be uncomfortable if he was still alive. It was a horribly traumatic experience (one that haunts me to this day) and the mortician's robotic, wordless demeanor only magnified my distress. I thought that this was what the death experience was supposed to be like. However, meeting Chelsea changed that. I learned through her stories that the man I met was the antithesis of what a funeral director/mortician should be. A true funeral director is someone who guides grieving people through the process, easing their way, and finding ways to comfort them when possible.

Deep down, I think all of us are curious about death, whether from morbid curiosity or fear of the unknown. My friends were entranced by Chelsea when they first met her and would ask questions rapid fire to sate their curiosity, but would often stop suddenly, occasionally with an apology, as if asking questions about death was taboo. It always amused me when they would exclaim to her, "But you seem so normal!" as if being a mortician meant she had to be a neurotic Elvira caricature. Even now, years later, many of them still ask her to tell them stories about what goes on in her chosen profession. We learned through her accounts that while death is usually tragic, the process of making final arrangements for a loved one doesn't need to be traumatic. Done right, it can be warm, comforting, transitional, and even fun under the right circumstances.

In this book, Chelsea introduces you into her version of the funeral industry. One that is governed by people who truly care for the living and the dead and take their profession very seriously. One where there can be joy and dancing mixed amidst tears and mourning. One where everyone can

Speaking of the dead by Chelsea L. Tolman

play a part in transitioning the dead to the afterlife, the ether, or nonexistence – all are welcome here.

Robert J. Labrum

November 2018

AUTHORS NOTE

This book contains my personal experiences and are recounted as I remember them. Death can be sad, funny and gross but most important of all, it is real. I encourage everyone to understand death as a part of life. It is going to happen and the more educated you are about the death industry, the more likely you are to make good decisions when it comes time to manage the death of someone you know.

Speaking of the dead by Chelsea L. Tolman

CONTENTS

Speaking of the dead by Chelsea L. Tolman

INTRODUCTION

I used to work in a junk yard. I loved the smell of grease and oil. The feel of the sun's heat in the desert as I walked around in full coveralls and steel toed boots, ripping out parts from mangled and junked trucks and vans, this was home for me. Until the day I called a mortuary.

Two of my coworkers had experienced deaths of close family members. I found myself listening to what they experienced at the funeral home, and not just the sadness and struggle with grief and loss but many times, in those few days, the mention of the funeral director was at the beginning of nearly every sentence, "The funeral director helped me with the obituary." "The funeral director helped me pick out flowers." "The funeral director said I should bring pictures." And more than just giving advice, they told me how kind and caring the funeral director had been in making the process easier, more manageable. I was fascinated by how this person "The funeral director" impacted their experience of losing someone they loved so intimately. It seemed the funeral director was better at comforting my friends than I was, and I had known them for years. They didn't know the funeral director personally, I didn't know the funeral director at all, yet this person, this stranger, gave so much weight to how my friends were getting through this beginning phase of loss that I was fascinated by it. So, I called a local mortuary and after short twenty-minute conversation, I hung up the phone and there was no doubt that my life was going to be different, I was going to be a funeral director.

I started my quest by visiting funeral homes and cemeteries. I asked questions, read literature and toured rooms filled with the dead on tables, in casket and in all stages of preparation. Now that I have some years under my belt, my career has affected me in so many ways. Meeting with the families of the recently deceased and preparing bodies for their final goodbye has given me an inside look of the funeral industry, now my industry, in a such an intimate way.

I met a man, now my husband, some years ago. As I met his family and friends the subject of my job would always come up. They were genuinely interested about the stories I told regarding my experiences as funeral director asking questions over a beer and rapt at the tales I had to tell. So I wrote my stories down and what I learned with each experience and now I am sharing these experiences and insights with the world. I want to bring the conversation about death and dying out into the open for all to understand that it

Speaking of the dead by Chelsea L. Tolman

is a part of us all. Embrace what you cannot control because ultimately, we are all going to die.

For those of you who have bought this book hoping to find gory tales of dismembered corpses and disturbing stories of macabre deeds, I'm afraid you're going to be disappointed. I feel very strongly that in any profession dealing with people's intimate moments, whether birth, life, or death, it is wrong for anyone to exploit their former clients in a disrespectful way, solely for the intent of earning money though sensationalism. There are of course people who will do so, but I choose not to join them. All of the stories I present to you here will never divulge the confidences of a family, disparage or disrespect the memory of any deceased person or describe the overall events in a disrespectful way. The events that take place in and in connection with a funeral home can be funny, terrifying, gross, sad, or horrifying. You may feel at first that I'm being uncaring in my descriptions of the events. However, understand that I hold all of these people and the memories associated with them in the highest regard because just as I played a role in shaping their lives at key moments, they did the same for me.

Speaking of the dead by Chelsea L. Tolman

This book is a collection of the stories that I have experienced personally. Most stories are told years after they happened, and they are described as my memory serves.

LIKE HYENAS

It was late in the evening maybe ten or eleven o'clock, well after sunset. The director and I had just "received" (picked up a person from someplace in mortuary lingo) a deceased man from his home and were now back at the mortuary where we transferred him to the embalming table. The director informed me that he was going out to get something to eat before he could get started on the preparations. I was still new at this and had not yet embalmed anyone by myself before. So, he gave me instructions to start the process and complete as much as I could on my own. In preparation, I tied my hair in a bun, suited up in my white embalming smock (like a chef's jacket), and adorned my surgical style white shoe covers. I grabbed two blue latex gloves, the same you would see in a hospital setting, from the box on the counter and repeated in my head "Two by two, hands of blue" (a homage to a TV show called Firefly that is one of my favorites) as I pulled the gloves over my fingers.

At this point I was comfortable "setting" features (closing the eyes and mouth for a pleasing, natural look) and "raising" blood vessels (finding the artery and vein needed for embalming), on my own so I knew I could complete this much while the director refilled his calories. The room was bathed in bright fluorescent lighting. I was surrounded by stark white walls and the white porcelain table bearing the dead man was in the center of the room with the foot end butted up against a set of white cabinets and counter-top, a sink, drain and the embalming machine. I pulled out the chemicals that were needed and lined them up next to the machine to wait until it was time to mix them.

I enjoyed this time of getting to know my patient. He was long and thin, a real "tall glass of water." He had brown hair that was mussed from being bed ridden and ill. He wore red sweat pants, a white t-shirt, and white socks that were stained and wrinkled from long wear. I carefully removed his clothing placing a towel over his private areas for modesty. He had died of Lou Gehrig's disease. I remember how his limbs were pulled unnaturally and his muscles and tendons were stiff, making it a task to straighten them out. I then spoke to him, telling him that once this part was over, his family would be grateful to see him at peace when they came to say their goodbyes. It was the first moment in what would become a natural routine for me, talking to the dead people in my charge. Maybe it was an attempt to give them, or me, some kind of comfort, maybe it was because I felt they deserved the kindness, the company. I don't know if the "spirit" stays with the body, but I know it felt like I should give this man some sense of acknowledgment because he had lived, and he was loved, even if his physical body was no longer working.

I kept talking as I worked, I told the dead man how beautiful his wife was and that she was going to have a hard time now that he was gone but she understood he had to go (all of these things I had witnessed when we were at his home). Once I had the man disrobed, I pulled out all of the instruments that were required for the procedure and laid them out neatly on the embalming table so that they were easily accessed when needed. I turned on the tap and directed the long hose from the sink to pour water down one side of the table. I washed the man's face with soap and fussed over closing his eyes and mouth so that he would look peaceful, at rest. I shaved the bit of stubble from his neck and chin making sure to get as close as possible without causing razor burn. Then I made the required incision and prepared the blood vessels for the embalming. Once I was finished with this, it had been about a half an hour already and the director had not yet returned.

Speaking of the dead by Chelsea L. Tolman

It was getting late, and I was sure the director would be back at any moment to help and manage things, so after waiting about ten minutes I became antsy to get finished and continued the process on my own. I mixed the chemicals and attached the hose of the embalming machine and flipped the switch to "on". As the machine moved fluid into the man's body, the gentle whir of its motor and the soft splashing of the water spilling from the hose were the only sounds in the room. I poured soap over his limbs and massaged his muscles, (this is to help facilitate blood flow and ensure that fluid is getting to all areas of the body.) I went slow and watched everything carefully by walking around from one side of the table to the other assuring that I wasn't missing anything. This process took me about an hour to complete and I was in the final stages of washing the body when the director walked into the room. I asked him if everything was okay, since he had been gone so long. He chuckled and revealed that he had meant for me to do this on my own all along. He walked up to the man on the table with a huge grin as he inspected and then praised my work. That was a proud moment for me, another test passed.

The next morning I walked into work, chest puffed out, head held high, remembering my big accomplishment from the night before. I was greeted by the funeral home manager as I walked in the door. Usually he was a jovial guy, always smiling and always ready with a witty joke. So, I was caught off guard when he walked up to me with purpose and a stern demeanor and immediately asked me, "Who embalmed Mr. so and so last night?" referring to the man I had prepared. I froze, then slowly in a meek tone of voice answered, "I did." He paused momentarily and then said, "Follow me." Immediately he turned on his heel and walked away without waiting for a response. As we walked down the long-carpeted hallway, the walls seemingly closing in on me the closer we got to the door of the embalming room, just like you see in bad horror movies. My head was reeling, what could have happened? I set the features, fluid was fine, body washed, cream on the face and hands, body covered with a sheet. I did all of it, just like I was supposed to.

As we entered the room the senior embalmer was already there waiting and standing over the man with his arms crossed. Oh man, I thought, this was serious! What did I miss? This is what a deflated balloon must feel like. One minute plumped up with air floating and bouncing happily with the breeze, then suddenly being stuck with a pin, popping the poor balloon leaving it to drift downward to end up as a seemingly sad, wrinkled lump on the floor. The fluorescent lights of the room felt hot, like the spotlight on a stage. Suddenly my suit was too tight and the air in the room heavy and hard to breathe in. Then with all of us standing in the room the sheet was pulled off of the table exposing the man that I had embalmed, all by myself, the night before.

Both men now had their arms folded standing next to the table and asked me to look at the man lying there and explain to them what was wrong. I did this, internally citing everything I had done right and seeing nothing abnormal, I had done a good job. So, I turned to them both with a newly gained confidence at seeing how well I had, I said "Nothing, there is nothing wrong with him." There was a moment of tense silence and then they both burst into laughter? Like a pair of hyenas they laughed, and I was so confused. Once these men were able to catch their breath I heard the most beautiful words, "Nope, there is nothing wrong with him, you did a great job!"

Speaking of the dead by Chelsea L. Tolman

HOW DO YOU DRESS A DEAD MAN?

I was a mortician-in-training walking with a coworker down the back hall of the mortuary towards the dressing room. Our task was to get a dead man dressed for a viewing scheduled for that evening. This would be the first body I had ever dressed. I imagined what this experience would be like. How does one possibly dress a dead person? I pictured wrangling clothing and limbs to pull on shirts and heft up pants on a person still and uncooperative. Having only been in school for a short while, I had no practical or hands on experience at all, so it was up to my imagination to envision how this task would be completed, until now.

My coworker opened the door to the room where our patient was waiting. Never before seeing a dead person up close without already having been prepared my nerves vibrated with anticipation, my stomach turns a bit at the reality that I am about to touch a dead person and then my resolve kicks in, I want to do this! As I walk through the doorway the man was lying on a cold, steel table covered to his armpits with a bright white sheet. Positioned so that his head was directed towards me and I was looking at a black mop of hair, freshly washed and combed.

Speaking of the dead by Chelsea L. Tolman

I look around the room, taking in my surroundings. The walls on all sides are a plain bright white. From the ceiling hang long fluorescent lights which illuminated every corner. Halfway between the floor and the ceiling on every wall around the space run a wooden trim board covered in gouges and scrapes, I assume these were caused by staff rushing about with tables and cots. On the wall to my left are white cabinets, starting from the floor and ending just before a cream-colored countertop stopped their progress. On each cabinet door, near the handle was a label announcing its contents. Makeup, plastics, waxes, polishes, and all sorts of chemicals needed for preparing the dead. The wall to my right is covered in metal shelving which holds pillows, sheets, blankets and other items needed for respectfully arranging a body for a family to see for the first time since the death occurred. The wall opposite the door I am standing in frames another door that entered the embalming room, a placard secured to the front of the door announced that it was a place for only those employed by the funeral home.

My coworker and I walk up to this man's body and discuss the procedure for getting him dressed. I am humming with excited energy that I am desperately trying to hold in, I didn't want my restless vibe to appear as nervousness that would lead me to be tagged the squeamish new girl. I am also aware of the slight glances my coworker laid in my direction, probably studying my reactions and how I was handling my first experience at being up close and personal with a dead man.

The family provided us with seven layers of clothing. Each layer is meant to signify a generation of descendants and the thickness of the layers corresponds the fullness of the life of the deceased. The family had lived in the United States for several generations yet still they incorporated their Chinese culture as they understood it. When I registered for mortuary college I had only limited experience with funeral customs. I only understood the traditional American funeral service which meant a night or two of visitation (when people would come to see the deceased and give condolences to the survivors), this was followed by a funeral in a chapel with pre-prescribed speakers and songs immediately trailed by a drive to the cemetery where there would be a committal service (blessing the ground and committing the body to the earth). The family would leave afterwards to partake in a meal and tell stories of the person they had just buried. However, this situation, is different.

Speaking of the dead by Chelsea L. Tolman

The seven layers of clothing is fascinating. I was told that the women in the immediate family would crawl on hands and knees crying and wailing their grief in raw uninhibited emotion and pretend money would be burnt in urns in the lobby. It was fascinating, this show of meaning and ritual. The concept that one layer of clothing could represent an entire generation of a family long past seemed romantic and meaningful. And why seven? Why not six or ten? And to have the worth of a life measured in thread count was both baffling and charming. I embraced this experience and additional enlightenment that we are products of ancestors. Bits of our past reside in our bones and these rituals come from ancestors long gone, a hint of that history in our behaviors, even generations later.

We had bags of clothing and we started pulling out pants and shirts and underwear and laid them on the countertops trying to decipher what went together. There was no indication of which layer was to go on first, or second or last, or if it even mattered. So, my coworker left the room to look over the paperwork again and get the proper instructions, leaving me alone with the dead man.

Speaking of the dead by Chelsea L. Tolman

I am standing in the center of the room and looked closer to the still and lifeless form on the table. Taking this precious opportunity to dig as far as I can in understanding what I had gotten myself into. I touch his arm, it was cold and felt harder than my own living tissue, his flesh didn't seem real but created from wax like a piece of art in a museum. I lower my face closer to his, I look at his lips, I study his eyelashes, eyebrows, the pores in his skin and in those few moments I know I saw him just sleeping. Like anyone would imagine a sleeping person to behave, I saw his chest raise up and down ever so slightly, his eye twitched just a hair as his dreams made him restless. But this is all just a trick of the eye, My imagination inserted the behaviors that are expected of a body lying down and eyes closed. He is not actually moving and twitching, and I understand that this is the first step in training my brain to recognize that death is certain and final.

I am not uncomfortable during this moment. People have reacted to my recounts of this experience with detest, even disgust. For me it is peaceful, calm, humble. I am excited to get more moments like this, moments that most people rarely experience. As a voyeur of the dead I wonder what really happens after we die. Are we transported to a black void? A mansion in the heavens? Given a new life? Or just stop, and experience nothing at all?

My coworker returned, and we proceed to dress the man in the correct order of layers. I am given instructions on how to stretch the shirt over the man's head without cutting it and lift his leg and thigh to get the pants all the way up to his hips, I am touched at how my coworker is so respectful, keeping the man's private parts covered until the first layer of clothing had been placed. At the third layer there wasn't any other choice but to start clipping the clothing up the back to get it to fit. The bulk of the previous layers unwilling to make room for the next. When all layers had been situated I reveled at how, even with all the bulk and fabric, the man still looked peaceful and natural.

My coworker announced that it was time to add cosmetics. I was shocked at this, the man looked so good already! His lightly brown skin was smooth, his lips had a natural color. I felt that adding cosmetics would only make him look... cosmetized. I was not in favor of changing this man's face and said as much. My coworker just chuckled, then took a small towel and tucked it into the collar of the dead man's shirt to protect it from getting stained as he worked. He told me to watch and invited me to ask questions if I had any. I observed as he applied the creams and powders and could not believe the transformation happening right before my eyes. Careful pats and dabs of color here and there and in no time the man looked much more alive than dead. I was learning cosmetic tricks in my college classes but to see it in action was a wholly different experience.

Once this was done and the now radiant looking dead man was ready for his funeral, we prepare his casket. This entails raising the casket mattress (a feature some caskets have - some raise and lower and tilt from side to side). We fluff the pillow for his head to rest upon. Then together with our arms we lift the man's body from the table and place him in his casket. I stand back and watch my coworker fuss over the details and all the layers. He straightened, tucked, tufted and arranged until he felt all was perfect. Then he steps back and stands next to me as we appraise his work. "Look good?" he asked "Looks perfect" I replied, and we left the room, satisfied of a job well done.

So many times, in the years after this first experience of dressing a dead man I have walked out of a room satisfied of a job well done. I was taught by some incredibly skilled and compassionate funeral directors and embalmers and have taken bits and pieces of advice and personality from all of them and combined this knowledge and skill with my own identity. Through doing this I have become my own creation, a skilled funeral director and embalmer built from ambition, determination and the knowledge of others. I revel in knowing that I have the skillset to help people during some of the most tragic and painful experiences they will ever go through.

NEVER A BRIDESMAID, NEVER A BRIDE

Death is a certainty. It comes in so many forms, ages and types. Young un-expected deaths are a difficult reality and young expected deaths can be even more difficult. When a child knows they are so sick that they are going to die before they get to drive, go to prom, have a first kiss or get married, the life they do experience carries more weight than for the rest of us. It becomes more about making the best of what you are given than to imagine what the future holds.

In this case it was a young girl, not yet thirteen. She had always been terminally ill. She knew that she would die young. She dreamed of doing the things that most girls her age do, like go to college or be a famous in some way. But what she wanted most was to be a bride, to wear the beautiful gown and have her hair curled and primped and be the center of attention for a day, her day. In the weeks before her death she told her mother that she wanted to be buried as the bride she had dreamed of being. She wanted to pick out her gown and looked at pictures of hairstyles. The girl had gotten to a point where she couldn't leave the hospital anymore, so her mother had a manicurist come to her room and apply pink

19

polish to her tiny, child hands. She died a couple of weeks later.

I remember meeting her mother. I remember her mother telling me how much her daughter wanted to be dressed like a princess in pink layers and lots of sparkles. I watched the pain and sorrow in the mother's eyes as she described her child's dream, knowing that she would never get to plan the wedding, or gain a son-in-law or grandchild, only that she would buy the casket that would accent the gown and make the arrangements for her daughter's funeral. We planned out the details and the family went home.

The next day the mother walked into the mortuary bearing her daughter's gown. She carried it like a child, like it was her most prized possession. Holding the hanger in one hand while the bulging plastic bag that protected the cherished dress draped over her other arm. Before she allowed me to take it from her hands, she told me the story of how she had spent the with her daughter shopping for the perfect dress, just weeks before she was permanently bed-ridden. She described to me how this young girl would try on dresses and giggle while turning around on the dress shop platform, admiring the flow of fabrics around her legs and watching her reflection in the tall mirrors. A mother's love is a powerful thing. For her to take her baby to wedding shops and endure the sidelong looks of the staff judging her for shopping for a wedding dress for one so young. Or have to answer, when questioned, that they were searching for a burial gown for this beautiful, young child. She watched and bore these moments that should have been for a planned wedding of a young woman and signify the beginning of a new life, not for the end of one.

I was given the dress which I carefully held in my arms in the same way mother had done. It was ceremonial, like passing a torch. After saying goodbye, I immediately went to the back rooms of the mortuary to uncover the dress wrapped in a plastic bag. It was a gown of pale cream with a hint of pink. The skirt had so many layers. Included was a slip that puffed with even more layers. The dress bore tiny bits of glitter nestled throughout the fabric that sparkled with every movement. The top was sleeveless and made of satin, the hint of pink gently peeking through when the light hit it just right. I hung it up on the back of a door and retied the bag to keep it protected.

The next day the beautician arrived at the mortuary. The girl was lying on a table in the center of one of our viewing rooms covered with a white sheet and on top of the sheet I had covered her with a burgundy blanket neatly folded over at her shoulders. Burgundy couches and dark wood end tables surrounded the room and stood against cream colored walls. I stayed in the room, watching as each curl was formed to become a lovely frame around the young girls' cherub face. Once finished, I thanked the beautician and walked her to the front door, then returned to the daughter, wheeled her into the back room once again and finished getting her ready.

Dressing this child was quite the experience. I wrestled with the layers that were designed to be placed on a bride who was standing up. Each layer had an agenda to move in its own direction and my attempt at forcing them to all behave in the manner I wanted, it would have been comical to watch I am sure. Layers snagged at my hair, flopped to the side and stuck straight up in the air, absolutely refusing to lay down properly. I finally had things arranged enough to finish the other details. With her hair neatly coifed and dress adorned I applied her makeup as her mother had instructed. Light powder, rosy cheeks, a hint of mascara and clear lip gloss was all that was needed.

Speaking of the dead by Chelsea L. Tolman

Her casket was a light pink, shiny and perfectly accented to the bits of pink fabric in her dress. A coworker and I wrestled with the rows of uncooperative layers as we lifted the child in our arms and gently laid her down on the soft mattress resting her head on the shiny satin pillow. I spent some more time arranging the dress, attempting to make it all fit inside the boundaries of the casket. This was not to happen. The pouf that surrounded and rose above the child's thin legs, spilled off the sides of its intended vessel, refusing to be corralled. I stood back from the casket and looked at the child and casket she lay in. The dress was meant to be seen, so I left the casket fully open, revealing the entire gown with her tiny feet peeking out from the bottom encased in thin, pink tights.

I had scheduled for the family to come and visit the child before the day of the funeral. Once they had all arrived, I had them gather in front of the door to the viewing room where the girl awaited their arrival, the mother stood in front of everyone and was clearly anxious. I explained what they would be walking into. It was the same room that I had led the beautician into just the day before, only now the girl lay in her casket against the right-side wall of the room. I explained that the casket was open to show off the glittery folds of the prized wedding gown.

Speaking of the dead by Chelsea L. Tolman

As I opened the door to the room and the family walked in, they were muted and subdued as they beheld the figure lying in a casket designed for those who had lived to grow old. I waited and listened as the silence turned to sniffles, then small cries and then the unforgettable wail of a grieving mother, a sound that hits your very heart and you will never forget. Wordlessly, I left the room to give them time to mourn in private and stood in the hallway just outside of the door for whenever I was needed.

A short time later the door cracked open and I was beckoned inside. The mother stood before me holding a pair of pale pink ballerina slippers. She explained that her daughter had taken ballet classes, so she thought the slippers were fitting and also, she wanted to be the one to place them on her daughters' feet but was afraid of doing it wrong or hurting her or breaking something. This is a common fear with people who are unfamiliar with the dead. She grabbed my hand and walked me to the foot of the casket, reluctantly letting my hand go as I talked her through what to do. Then we placed a halo of little white embroidered flowers with yellow centers around the crown of the girl's head, and she truly looked like an angel. The moment was precious, and I watched her mother's heart break as she prepared to bury her child bride.

AND THEN THERE WAS DANCING

I have been fortunate to witness many rich and beautiful funeral rituals and customs. For a time, I worked for a funeral home that was located in a region where several different cultures lived close by, and I was able to witness many of these funeral traditions. One that I will never forget was the first funeral from an African region that I was an assistant on.

My tasks for this funeral included making sure the "behind the scenes" details were handled, emptying trash cans as they filled with tissue and refilling the toilet paper and hand towels in the bathrooms. I was also to be in charge of the music, hitting the play button at the right time and stop when each song was over.

As the family and guests started arriving, I was mesmerized with the beautiful robes of bright colors and heavy fabrics that were wrapped and adorned with so much care. Almost every person was wearing a head dress of some sort, oranges and yellows in stained glass type patterns. And every person walked with purpose and confidence and grace and the whole building had an air of peace that was warming and friendly.

I was so enamored with the living people that I do not remember the one in the casket. I was given my marching orders, the written-out details of the program firmly gripped in my hand with instructions like when to be at the back of the chapel to greet and seat the guests, when to make sure the center aisle was clear for the entrance of the casket and the order in which the songs were to be played in during the service.

Once the guests and family were settled I entered a separate room located in the back of the chapel. This was the music room which had a large glass window and speakers allowing me to watch and listen to what was happening during the service. I queued up the music and situated myself in my chair. Next to me sitting on a stool next to me was a guitar player. As she turned the knobs of her guitar, tuning it up and plugging into the music system, we talked a little. Then we were ready, and the service began, and I hit my buttons as the program instructed.

Speaking of the dead by Chelsea L. Tolman

As I hit play for the second song in the program, suddenly the back of the chapel came alive with twirling colors of blue and orange and yellow. I stood up from my chair and blinked my eyes to better see what was happening. As I watched three women in flowing dresses gracefully danced up the aisles to the front of the chapel, perfectly in time to the melody I was playing for them. In picture-perfect unison, the dancers' dresses waved with the long, fluid movements of their arms and legs. I sat back down and watched with wonder in my little music room, grateful for the glass window allowing me to see this. I heard a soft chuckle from the woman on the stool. I pulled my eyes from the dancers to look at her only to see that she was chuckling at me. With a huge smile she explained the dance and how it told a story that honored the deceased and the family.

When the funeral was over, my next task was to instruct the pall bearers on how to safely carry the casket. I stood in the doorway that led to the waiting hearse. I stood in my "funeral" posture, straight-backed, hands together in front of me, looking straight ahead. It was what I had learned was professional for our industry. I stood this way patiently waiting for all of the gentlemen to line up in front of the door. One pallbearer, who was standing to my right, decked out in bright yellows, gold and browns looked at me with interest and said, "Why are you so sad?" Shocked at the comment I looked at him confused. He continued, "This is a happy day, you get to honor someone who has died."

I had never viewed my job in this way. All of the funeral directors I worked with carried the same somber face, not happy, not sad, just present and I just emulated them, thinking this was how you were supposed to carry yourself as a funeral director. I learned so much in that one man's comment. I don't always have to take a somber stance when honoring the dead, it is a privilege to serve families and they deserve real interactions. Death is real, the families are real and I, as a funeral director, should be real. It is a happy day that I get to honor those who have died. I vowed from that day on to serve my families with that exact sentiment. Sometimes there are tears, sometimes there is laughter and then sometimes there is dancing.

Speaking of the dead by Chelsea L. Tolman

EMPTY CHAPEL

This may be a strange thing to say but I have been witness to some very sad funerals. That is not to say they aren't all sad in their own way. My perception of a sad funeral isn't necessarily how the family or others view it either. My goal as a funeral director is to help the family create a service that reflects the person who died, invite family and friends to attend and ensure that all the details are handled from the visitation to the burial or cremation. Success on these fronts is a positive experience in that the goal was accomplished and the family can begin some kind of closure. When things do not go as planned and the family does not receive the service they want or the closure they need, it is undoubtedly sad.

One funeral I was helping with was for a woman who had died fairly young, late fifties I would guess. She had only one daughter and she had come in by herself to arrange her mother's funeral. She was to have a chapel service at the funeral home and burial in a local cemetery. She had already selected her casket, indicated the clergy who would officiate, and she had also chosen her burial gown, more accurately burial nightgown complete with soft pink slippers. She was not going to have a public viewing, so it seemed appropriate that she be dressed for comfort.

I remember getting this woman dressed. Her nightgown was made of soft fuzzy fabric, pale cream with little blue and pink scattered all over it. And it covered her from neck to ankles including long sleeves. The slippers were a sturdy pink satin with thick, squishy cushioned soles the kind that cradles your feet as you walk. After getting her gown and slippers placed, I brushed out her long hair, it was a muted blonde color with streaks of grey and white. The color that clearly defines the beginning transition from middle age to senior. After combing the long locks I twisted the strands together to form a tight, neat bun on the top of her head. She had no cosmetics aside from a light pink gloss on her lips. She felt calm and peaceful, I believe that she had suffered in life and now imagined that she was finally at rest.

The daughter came in alone the day before the service to see her mother. I walked her into one of the viewing rooms. The gray metal casket was placed against one wall, and torchier lamps (tall thin lamps that are used for lighting at the ends of the casket) standing and lit on both ends. The casket lid was open and the daughter walked inside the room. I left the room to give her time alone with her mother. I never saw when she left, she had quietly snuck out without a word and no one saw her.

I had everything ready on the day of the service, I set out printed programs and a customized register book. There were pictures in the chapel and the clergy had arranged an order of service. There was only one song to be played which would signify that the service was over. There were only two speakers, the clergy and the daughter. It was getting closer and closer for the funeral to start, and there were no guests! Not one person arrived aside from the daughter, the clergy and the funeral staff. I was getting worried that something was wrong, so I ran to the back office and checked the obituary to make sure the time and location was right, and yes everything was in order and had been printed correctly. I checked again the list of survivors, she had siblings and nieces and nephews, yet, no one was there. I thought to myself that there was no way that not one person, aside from the daughter, would be at this woman's funeral!

Baffled, I went to speak with the clergy and asked how well he knew the other family members, he stated that he was not surprised that no one else was there but would not elaborate further. I asked him about any friends who should be there, he said he didn't know of any personally. The daughter was calm and smiling and didn't seem at all affected by the fact that the chapel was empty. She acted as if it was the most normal day and that no one was supposed to be there anyway. So, I chose not to bring it up unless she did so first.

We all played our part in starting the service, my coworker and I wheeled the casket into the empty chapel, the clergy sat up front next to the pulpit and the daughter was seated alone in the front row. My coworker and I made our exit and gave a brief look to each other and I left while the service took place. The average funeral service lasts about forty-five minutes, even a very short service is still good thirty minutes. So, funeral directors normally use this time to do other things. I walked to the back offices and started a fresh pot of coffee, then used the restroom. I thought I should check and see where things were in the program since I had planned to sit in the back of the chapel while the daughter spoke, giving her even the smallest of audience.

As I rounded the corner to where the back doors of the chapel were, I noticed that the doors were wide open (normally the chapel doors stay closed during a funeral service). Then as I got closer two of my coworkers made their way out of the chapel with the casket! I was gone no more than ten minutes and this entire funeral service was over? The sad procession of three, including the deceased, made their way out of the doors and to the waiting hearse. I stood momentarily frozen in shock. This was by far the shortest funeral service in my experience of funeral services.

I said that it was sad because this poor daughter memorialized her mother by herself, with no friends, no other family, and only the clergy had shown up. I will never know why no one else was there but I can say that even when her mother was lowered into the ground, this daughter never acted like she wasn't surrounded by friends and family. Maybe it wasn't sad for her and maybe it was and she just didn't show it, or maybe the sadness was only my perception and memorializing this woman alone is just what the family had agreed to and what daughter needed. I will never know for sure but will always remember the big empty chapel.

TIMING IS EVERYTHING

I was sitting in the arrangement room with a family when the wife of the deceased told us she wasn't feeling well. The poor woman was the color of putty and had to take several bathroom breaks. I was concerned and asked if she wanted to wait until the next day to go through this. She declined and kept saying, "It's just nerves, I will be fine". So, I brought her some crackers and a sprite, hoping it would settle her stomach. We continued with the arrangements and I had it planned that everything that could be done on the phone and through email was left for last and then told the family to take the wife home to rest, that I would be in touch for the final details.

The next day I called the house to check on her, a family friend answered the phone and told me that the wife had been sleeping a lot but still had a sour stomach, getting sick a couple of times during the night. She also told me that the wife kept insisting that she would feel better once her husband was buried. With this information, I planned for the limousine to have plenty of sprite and a bag of pretzels and a freshly laundered blanket for her. Even with this, I was completely unprepared for what was going to happen!

Speaking of the dead by Chelsea L. Tolman

On the day of the service, my apprentice was to pick up the family in the limousine at their house and bring them back to the funeral home for a formal procession to the church. I was waiting at the funeral home, the hearse was loaded with the man in his casket, the police escorts were all in place, we were just waiting for the family. Families are almost never prepared when the limousine shows up, for one reason or another. Someone has to run back in the house for a purse or the speech they prepared. And then once one person has gone back inside, someone else suddenly remembers something important that they must go retrieve. So, sometimes it can take longer than planned to get the family out of the house and into the limousine, so it wasn't a surprise when they didn't show up on time.

Finally, the police escort was getting antsy and approached me to ask when we were going to leave, when the limousine thankfully pulled into the parking lot, driving faster than normal. The limousine driver was a young apprentice whom I had hired just a couple of months beforehand and as the car got closer, through the windshield, I could see she had a look of horror on her face! I waited until the car stopped to approach but before I could get to the drivers' door to talk to her, the back doors suddenly flung open and people scrambled out, running for the doors of the mortuary! I was confused. I asked what was going on. Apparently, the wife was not sick with nerves, she was sick with a terrible stomach bug and had given it to all of her family members! It was explained to me that they were so late because several people had to go back into the house, which only had one bathroom, to empty their stomachs.

Now, judge me if you want but I found this entire scenario to be a funny. Like a comedy movie where the family is stumbling over each other to be sick yet insisting to get on with the funeral. I empathized for the family and was saddened that they were so sick but still it was all I could do to not laugh out loud. So, after evaluating the situation, I approached one of the daughters as she came back to get in the car and told her that it was completely appropriate and understandable to postpone this funeral for a day or two and that everyone, including me, would appreciate not being exposed to the germs.

The family gathered and talked about it and decided that no, there would be a funeral today and they were all going to be there, even the ones who were to speak! "Ugh, okay, let's do this", was what I said, but only in my head.

Speaking of the dead by Chelsea L. Tolman

Eventually we all piled in our cars and began the drive to the church. About halfway to there, I noticed the limousine behind me slowing down and then pull off to the side of the road. The police escort ahead of me was not slowing down so I decided to continue on with the escort, at the very least I could get the casket there and in place to be ready when the family arrived.

Once I got to the church, I approached the clergy and told him what was going on, apparently, he found this to be just as funny as I did. Not in a rude way, just that it was such bad timing! I asked the clergy to make an announcement to the guests seated in the chapel and inform them that the service was going to run later than it already was and to let them know what the family was dealing with. I wrangled some of the men in the crowd and together we were able to get the casket into the chapel. After some time, the limousine finally pulled into the church parking lot, this time at normal speed.

The family was exhausted, and my apprentice was exasperated, and visibly shaken at having to negotiate the two stops they had to make and find her way to the church with a carload of sick people but, I did not have the time to console her just yet. I again asked the family if they wanted to postpone and again, they insisted on having this funeral.

It is a necessity that, in funeral service, we handle some uncomfortable tasks. Tasks that most people wouldn't even consider doing, yet, most of the time, these things do not take place at the church! The limousine had a pile of vomit from a time when the car couldn't pull over fast enough and I had to charge my young apprentice with the ghastly task of cleaning the mess while I handled the family and service. The girl complied with shaky hands and tear-filled eyes, stating she just wanted this day to be over with. I sympathized with her but there was nothing else to be done about it and left her to the chore, escorting the family to the chapel and getting them seated.

Most of the time during a service I will sit in the lobby and listen to what is taking place, this gives me time to make phone calls and arrange other things that need to be handled, yet, every once in a while, like with this situation, I will sit in the back of the chapel to get a better handle on what was happening in case I needed to react quickly. During the service the family members each in turn stood and hastily sidled past all the people in the pew to rush off to the restroom. Then upon return, sidled through the pew again to reclaim their seats. Up and down, scoot and sit. It was a constant coming and going from one family member to another back and forth through the entire service.

Normally after a service, the family is swarmed with guests, greeting them and giving condolences yet, today, once the service was over, the guests kept their distance, waving from afar and letting the family make their getaway quickly out of the chapel. I approached the family again and this time I didn't ask, just simply stated that it was best for them to go home and let us bury the man without them. Then when they felt better they could go visit the grave. They were so exhausted, they thankfully agreed, and once again, my apprentice had to get in the car with the sick family and take them home while I drove the casket to the cemetery. The man was buried successfully, and I met my apprentice back at the funeral home to console her and praise her for her efforts.

In this situation, there wasn't much else we could do but support the family in their decision to trudge through the day. I hope the church got a thorough cleaning and thankfully none of my staff caught the bug. The timing of this family's illness was terrible, but we did the best we could and got through it.

Speaking of the dead by Chelsea L. Tolman

YOU DON'T KNOW WHAT YOU DON'T KNOW

As I was writing this book I was reminded of families that I have served who are under the impression that they don't need a ceremony or a service to commemorate a loved one. Some feel that they can move on by doing something with the body and then continuing on with their life. It's not that easy. Loss needs to be experienced. It should be felt in all it's beautiful and horrible ways. When your heart it shredded like fraying fabric and dangling in pieces, the scotch tape method isn't going to work long term. Careful stitching and honest grieving is necessary to put things back into place. Maybe not perfectly, but at least in a way so you can breathe again.

There was a young man (late twenties) who died in his apartment of a drug overdose. He had moved away from his family and had been living in a different state for several years. He had made a life here with new friends, rarely connecting with his family. When he died, his father flew in to make the arrangements.

I was waiting in the lobby when the father walked in with his wife (not the young man's mother) and greeted them as they entered. The father was stoic and unemotional, indicating that he wanted to get this business over with and leave the funeral home. So I walked them to the room where we would sit and talk about the plans for the young man's services.

I began by asking about his son. What was he like? What were his hobbies? But was quickly interrupted. The father stated that he would sign the necessary paperwork for the cremation and pay the bill. Then they had a flight scheduled for the next morning to go back home. I explained to him that the process would take longer than that (there are permits to get, the crematory had a schedule, those types of things) and also to let him know that he should consider spending some time with his son before he was cremated, especially since he had not seen him in such a long time. But he didn't want to hear any of it. His father, who was understandably grief stricken, said he wanted to cremate his son and go back to his home state. He even suggested that he could sign the paperwork and have me mail the ashes to his house! I continued to listen. He told me that he did not know his son anymore. He had made friends that the father had never met, he worked several jobs and bounced around living situations. The father's solution was to bury himself in life and forget that his son had died, making the comment that it wouldn't be any different than things were right now anyway.

So I changed the direction of the conversation. I asked about the vitals (legal information, social security number, date of birth etc.) that I would need for the death certificate. The father's wife was silent through this process. She never spoke or gave an opinion yet, her countenance perked up when I mentioned a service, seeing the body, anything that meant more than just a cremation. We had some silent moments when our eyes locked in mutual concern that the father was really needing more than to run away from this one shot opportunity at seeing his son and commemorating his life.

I continued asking more questions, "Are there other siblings?" No. "Is there a biological mother living?" No. "Does he have many friends where you live, where he grew up as a child?" Not really. Then it stands to reason that if this man wanted to know his son, wanted to understand what kind of life he lived and who he lived it with, it would be here, in the place that the young man had made his home. I casually suggested that he have an open floor memorial (an informal type of service, where only friends and family would come to the microphone and speak, nothing else preplanned). We could print an obituary with this information in the paper and then I suggested that he stay here and see who showed up to tell the story about his son. My purpose in suggesting this was that the father could be wrong. The young man's friends and coworkers might not all be bad influences and even more than that, they should get the chance to say goodbye and have some kind of closure.

Immediately, he got angry. He pointed out that his sons' roommates, friends and coworkers were likely the cause of his overdose and he had no intention of seeing or speaking to any of those people. He was going to cremate his son and leave. His reaction was my queue to leave it alone. He had the right to just take his son home. We signed the paperwork, he paid the bill and him and his wife went home.

The next morning, I was sitting at my desk arranging for other funerals when I received a call from the fathers' wife, they wanted to do as I suggested. They wanted an obituary printed and asked me to put together a memorial for the young man. I told her I was happy that they changed their minds and I would start making the arrangements right away. Then the father got on the phone and told me he is sure that no one would show up but in the case that one person who loved his son was there, it was only fair to let them say their peace. I agreed with him, we set a day and time, said goodbye and I hung up the phone.

My heart fluttered, I was so excited! I wrote the obituary and emailed it to his father for input. I planned with the father to have the service at a venue where there could be food and drinks and tables to sit at. The microphone would be located an area easily accessible for any who wanted to stand and speak. I then busied myself with all of the other details. I asked the father to send me digital pictures of his son, which I then printed out and placed in frames.

On the day of the service I set up a long table in the room where people could look at the framed pictures of the young man, They were pictures from his younger years before he moved away and all outdoor poses, next to a stream or sitting on the side of a huge rock. He was smiling in them, it was a wonderful display of a vibrant, happy child. I had notecards and pens sitting out for friends to write notes or personal stories that the father could take home with him. The tables were covered in brilliant blue table cloths and each had a bowl of succulents sitting in the center. I made sure the caterer was on time and placed the urn on a tall round table next to the microphone.

The father and his wife showed up early. As they walked towards me the father's shoulders were hunched. He seemed nervous, hesitant, and I presume pessimistic of anyone showing up. As he looked around the room and saw the pictures of his son smiling and happy in photos of years when they went hiking and fishing together, he slowly relaxed and exclaimed how everything in this room reflected his son as he once knew him and commented on the thoughtfulness of the whole arrangement. Him and his wife walked around, looking at the pictures, the food set out and the urn patiently waiting next to the microphone.

Not long after, a single person walked in. I greeted him and asked the relation, a friend, so I introduced him to the father. Then more people showed up. Small groups entered the room, walked around the long table, wrote on the notecards and spoke to the father. Eventually the room was full. I walked up to the microphone and encouraged people to get a plate of food and find a seat at a table, and then it was time to start.

Speaking of the dead by Chelsea L. Tolman

Getting people to stand up to a microphone in front of a crowd is always a challenge. It is a type of game convincing people that it isn't scary to bare your soul in front of others. I introduced myself and the father (him and his wife sat at a table in the back of the room). I explain as I talked, that everyone in the room should think of their friend and what made him special, "Get ready to tell your story" I said. Then I spoke about what I knew, the things his father had told me about the young man, how I would have liked to know this kid in life and the only possible way was through them, the people who worked, lived and played alongside him.

Then I opened the floor for others "The first person gets a free drink" I said... chuckles (they were already free), then silence. Then one person stood up and made his way to the mic and told a story of his friend. Tears, laughter and pockets of silence as people slowly made their way to the mic and told stories about their friend. People kept coming up and the stories were the same. They talked about how this young man had changed their lives, how he had made them feel special, how they tried to help him through his addiction. He was a support to everyone in the room. Even more, in the evenings he had volunteered for a drug rehab center, coaching people who were fighting their own addiction. These people loved him, they missed him, and they wanted him back. So many people spoke directly to the father and thanked him for giving them the opportunity to tell their story of who their friend was, it was healing, and it was beautiful.

Then, when no one else was coming up to the mic, the father got up, slowly, shaking, and made his way to the front of the room. I handed him the mic and he stood there for a moment and looked around the room with tear-filled eyes. It took several seconds to get his composure, to make any sound from his throat. Then, he talked. He talked about his son and how he was heartbroken when he moved away from home. How he worried everyday if he was alive or dead. He talked about the conversations he had with his son when he knew he was high on drugs and would fear for him and ache for his safety. Then he talked about the people in this room. He explained his initial plan was to cremate his son quickly and just leave but decided at the last minute to change his flight home and arrange for this service and now he was glad that he did. He thanked everyone for showing up, for helping and loving his son who struggled so much. He thanked them for telling him how much his son helped them, that there was a purpose in his son building a life here. How all of their words have begun to heal the anger and sadness he felt over his son's death, that there was now a lightness in knowing that for all these years, his son was surrounded by caring and loving people and he hadn't carried the burden of fearing for his son alone.

When he finished, there was not a dry eye in the room. I took the mic back and thanked everyone for coming then closed the service. Some people left right away but some stayed and hugged the grieving father. The box of written notecards was filled to the brim. The stories that were shared were immense and heavy and the father, who thought he lost his son years ago to people who weighed him down, now knows they were actually a pillar of strength and encouragement and that his son was loved and cradled up until the end. While the father chose not to see his son's body, the healing that came from this simple ceremony had changed years of imagining what his son's life had been like. You just don't know what you don't know.

GRABBED BY A DEAD MAN

People have asked me how a dead body reacts once it is dead. I do not mean to refer to the dead as an "It" in a disrespectful way, I am purposefully taking the human element out of the conversation. What I mean is, I get asked questions like "Do they sit up?" "Do they moan?" "Do the dead do living human things after they are dead?" I have also been asked, do you get scared, or creeped out or have had an experience that makes you want to scream or run or quit? The answer to the first question is no, people do not sit up on their own unless they are still alive. It takes flexing muscle to sit up and after the body has died there is no communication from the brain to tell the muscle what to do. Yes, they do moan but only on occasion and even then they have to be physically moved, air trapped in the lungs can escape through the lips to create a sound like moaning or sighing. The industry calls this a "death moan". I have known funeral directors to compress the chest and get the moan out before they place the body on a gurney, just so they don't have to experience this unexpectedly. As far as doing living human things, to be blunt, dead bodies alleviate their bowels and bladders. Not all the time but frequent enough. This happens when all of the muscles in the body have relaxed, it just is what it is. So, if the

51

body cannot move on its own after it is dead, how then does one become grabbed by a dead man?

It was late at night and dark outside. I had just returned to the mortuary with my passenger who was lying on the cot peaceful and very still, not at all grabby. The family requested for him to be embalmed, so I took the necessary steps to prepare. I placed him on the embalming table. The room was lit by bright fluorescent lights reflecting off of stark white walls and the white porcelain embalming table sat in the center. I disrobed the man and started my other prep work. Part of my preparation ritual was to find a good radio station, it is comforting to have music in the background when it is just you and the dead, in the dark of night, alone. So, with Stevie Ray Vaughan playing in the background, embalming instruments out and ready, the man on the table with his arms lightly folded on his belly. I begin the work of closing his eyes and mouth and silently pleading with him to give me a pleasant expression, when out of the corner of my eye I saw a small movement and then suddenly wham! The man's hand had grabbed my leg!

I froze, to myself, in my head I said "Don't react, don't jump or scream". I am still… like a mouse… trying to assess what the heck was going on. I slowly looked down and sure enough the dead man's arm was hanging from the table and gripping my thigh. It does seem a tad bit silly now, because the man was not alive, he did not move to accost me on his own. In my concentration, my movements of the table while getting him ready simply knocked his loosely placed arm off of the table and onto my leg and due to his rigor mortis, his hand was already in a curled position that just happened to fit perfectly around my thigh. This does happen, when the muscles of the body no longer work, they tend to slide and slip if not secured in some fashion and end up in places they were not intended. Woe is me and the hurdles I must face when preparing a grabby dead man.

CAN I GET A SECOND OPINION?

Before I tell this story, I want you all to know that the majority of people I meet take way too much stock in Hollywood's versions of dead bodies and what they do, or do not do, in the days before they are buried or cremated. I have had people tell me about the bodies that sit straight up, "I saw it with my own eyes!" Or watched a woman in a casket breathe, or blink, or twitch a finger, or whatever their eyes told them happened. It's true that our minds decide what we see, that the dead are not dead, there was a mistake and they are still breathing just really slowly, "Just like in that show I saw" people have told me. I have been brought back into a room where the family frantically asks me to call a doctor because so and so opened their eyes for split second, or their mouth twitched "I swear I saw it". I don't mean to make light of these situations because it's traumatic and sad. The truth is, unless you are around the dead all day, our minds are trained to see a person sleeping. Sleeping people twitch and breath and move, combine that normalcy with the yearning for the person to still be alive and hope to not have to handle the loss in the coming days and years can assuredly create false impressions of movement. It is heart wrenching and I have to calmly explain to the family that they are seeing things that

54

are not there and assure them that their deepest wish is not going to come true.

The hardest of these moments for me was a young girl who lost her mother unexpectedly. She was probably in her early thirties and an only child. She had not been close to her mother in recent years and there was a ton of unresolved anger and sadness that turned to guilt when she died. The daughter was unmarried, her father estranged, and there was no other family to support her.

When she came in to see her mother's body, she brought with her four of her friends for support, one of them a hospice nurse. I walked them into the large viewing room, the lights were slightly dimmed, and the woman lay on a table covered to her shoulders with a sheet. The daughter was rightly upset, and emotion overtook her as the girls stepped up to the body. I felt the daughter had all the support she needed so I stepped out into the hallway to give them time alone, letting one of her friends know that I was right outside the door if they needed anything.

It took less than a minute for one of the girls to burst through the door into the hallway practically yelling, "Call

911, she is still alive!" and "Call a doctor quick!" I have to say that I was only surprised because one of these girls was a hospice nurse. She should know that dead bodies don't come back to life funeral homes. Yet, this is what happened, and the girls were most assuredly feeding off of each other's frantic energy.

I calmly walked her back into the room and listened as they all told me the same story of an eye twitch. I thought it best to look the woman over again myself in an effort to look like I was investigating the situation, but she was just as still as before, not at all twitchy. I turned around and addressed the girls while standing next to the dead woman explaining to them what they were or, more accurately, were not seeing. To give context, the woman had not been embalmed, there would not be a service and she was to be cremated later that day.

I remember the daughter's reaction as if it happened yesterday. She turned to me with clear, bright blue tear filled and hopeful eyes as she argued that maybe the doctors got it wrong "Can you please just call?" she pleaded. My heart ached for her. Her pain was real and tangible. She argued where had seen a TV show where a dead person was only in a coma that made them appear dead and then later came back to

Speaking of the dead by Chelsea L. Tolman

life. So, after more explanation of the trickery of our eyes and helping them understand the real, hard truth, the girls finally calmed down. The daughter slumped her shoulders and hung her head in resignation and I asked her friends to come into the hallway with me and leave the daughter to have a final conversation with her mom and hopefully resolve some of the guilt that she will undoubtedly struggle with for the rest of her life.

Speaking of the dead by Chelsea L. Tolman

BALLOONS

Balloons, gently floating up through the clouds with their ribbon tails softly swaying in the breeze. It's a back and forth, soft bumping and rocking type of event. It used to be common for graveside services to have the crowd release balloons in homage to the deceased. The practice is slowly fading and even banned in some areas, thankfully, due to the damage they cause to the environment and wildlife after they deflate and fall to the ground. This experience that I am about to relate is not a recent event, just a beautiful memory.

With every balloon release I am mesmerized, watching them drift up and away, like it was the first time I had ever seen it. There is an excitement in trying to keep track of your single balloon as it gets smaller and smaller while everyone around you secretly urges their own balloon on, hoping it will rise higher and faster than anyone else's. Often, I will hand out Sharpie markers and watch as the crowd struggles to hold a balloon in the crook of their arm or between their legs as it fights for release. There is a hollow screeching concert of marker on rubber as people write out loving messages for someone, most believe, is up above in the heavens. It is also inevitable that one or two balloons get away before the countdown is made to let them go. And almost every time, the Sharpies' squawking stops and heads turn upwards to watch the rogue balloon float away with a background of murmurs stating the obvious faux pas of the individual who didn't hold to their string tight enough. Sometimes it's an adult who lost their battle of holding onto a balloon while writing their heartfelt note, sometimes it's a child not understanding how helium works, and a lot of times there are tears at the lost opportunity to have this balloon sent on its way up, alongside the multitude.

One funeral in particular that I directed was for an infant, a baby boy. Before he was born, the family knew he was going to die shortly after birth. These are heartbreaking funerals and they must be handled in a very delicate way. The spot in the cemetery that the family had purchased pre-need (before a death occurs) was a garden still under construction and was not quite ready for burials at the time of the infant's death. In this case, we planned a small ceremony at an above ground crypt where the infant would be placed and held until the new garden was open. At that time we would move him to the previously planned location.

Speaking of the dead by Chelsea L. Tolman

I had everything ready at the crypt before the family and friends were to arrive. It was a drizzly day, not quite raining, yet but wet and dark grey skies threatened a downpour. It was a short walk from the road to an alcove walled on two sides with cream colored marble crypts reaching high above our heads and a large tiered concrete fountain in the center happily splashing water over its sides. The other two sides of the area looked out over the expanse of the cemetery lawn dotted with huge trees full of green leaves, heavy with moisture. I placed a small table for the tiny casket to rest upon during the service. The flower van was parked nearby against a curb the back end full of light blue balloons awaiting their liberation. I parked the dark blue limousine near the curb of the walkway that led to alcove and just inside its back door, the seat held a small white casket cradling the precious baby boy's body.

As people arrived, I busied myself with opening their car doors and holding out umbrellas, assuring that everyone was as comfortable and as dry as possible. Once the family was ready and it was time to start the funeral, the father and brother of this tiny human lifted the casket from the back seat of the limousine and hand carried him with a slow, careful walk to the alcove and the awaiting crowd. The grieving mother paced close behind. Large black umbrellas jounced in the hands of the audience as they all tried to find enough space to watch and listen to those who were speaking.

After the ceremony, everyone gathered behind the flower van. The Sharpies were handed out and one by one the blue balloons were passed around and then, just as I handed out the last balloon, it started to rain! Not a downpour, but enough drops to make the task of releasing balloons a difficult one. As friends and family began writing their messages, the squeal of marker on rubber permeated the heavy air around us. Most everyone huddled under umbrellas in an attempt to keep the raindrops from ruining their valuable drawings and messages. Coat sleeves and long dresses were used to towel off the rubber spheres when drops found their way past the umbrella canopy. Then, with smeared marker messaged balloons, the crowd walked down the road of the cemetery to where the baby boy would ultimately be interred, leaving the crypt where the cemetery crew would complete the task of closing in the tiny casket.

It was a somber, walking procession of family and friends along the empty road of the cemetery. Grass and trees lining both sides of the street we walked on. As we reached our destination there was a last attempt at wiping the moisture off of the balloons and then they were released into the thick, soggy air. Some of the balloons lifted enough to rise but most just lazily wafted in the slight breeze, heavy with rain drops, only to dive just a few feet away or hover over the newly seeded grass. Children and adults alike would gently walk over the tiny sprigs of new grass to grab a rebellious balloon, wipe off the offending drops and hurl it upwards as best they could. After every failed attempt was made, the crowd finally dispersed leaving behind a pasture of sadly grounded baby blue balloons.

Some weeks later we got the go-ahead to open the new garden and we could finally put the baby boy in his final resting place, so we arranged another graveside service. We planned to take the tiny casket from the crypt and walk down the cemetery road to the grave, say a few words and release a new bundle of balloons. This day was beautiful and sunny and no rain in sight. Blue skies, bright green trees and grass, everything was perfect! The family started gathering at the crypt and I was busy getting all of the things ready, including securing another collection of balloons at the new gravesite. I set up a table with pictures, markers and handouts, then began securing the balloons to the table leg. I made a knot in the

Speaking of the dead by Chelsea L. Tolman

bundle of strings, making sure they were secure and then I let go, and then, so did the balloons! I froze for a second, confused, then launched myself up desperately grabbing at the strings that quickly rose out of my reach. In seeming slow motion I turned my head towards where the family was gathering and saw that every head was arched upwards to watch the balloons float up and away.

I was certain that the family would be crushed – first the balloons that wouldn't fly and now this! As I walked down the road to talk to the family, I made a call to the shop where I got the balloons and explained what had happened and that I needed more balloons delivered right away!

To my surprise and great relief, the family was laughing when I reached them. They all exclaimed at how much fun it was to see the balloons lift off in one big bundle and then watch my horrified face as I tackled the air attempting to get the balloons back to the ground.

In the end we did get more balloons, and everything else went as planned. The family had a surprise though. They had returned to the cemetery after the last service and collected the balloons that had fallen. We tied the deflated, marker smeared balloons to some of the new ones, allowing their journey to continue. My lesson from that day was that even when everything, from my perspective, seemed to be going wrong; the grass not ready for burial, the need for two services for the infant, balloons that would not rise in the rain to the second set of balloons launched before the ceremony could start, even after all of that, this family made the best of it. They cherished the moments as part of the process and instead of things being a disaster, every step of it was made beautiful. With the right attitude almost everything has significance, even long deflated, marker smeared balloons.

MISSING TOE

There was a preacher in this small town that I worked in who officiated a good many of our funerals. He was a round man with a kind and gentle expression, he always greeted you with a jovial smile and ready with a good one liner or silly story. Everyone knew him well and loved him for the remarkable person that he was and the good he did for others. He was always seen with a two-piece suit and bow tie of bright colors and interesting patterns. His wife, who was just as kindhearted, handmade his bow ties and her own dresses to match them, they were almost always together, always matching. He was a bigger man and you can imagine that equates to not being in the greatest of health. Of course, this was a small southern town where vegetables meant boiled cabbage drenched in sauce or butter and corn on the cob dripping with margarine and salt. Southern barbeque is always served with a plate size serving of corn bread slathered in honey butter, the mom and pop diners dished out grand helpings of biscuits and gravy complete with platters of thick, crispy bacon. Good ole fashioned southern food fried, drenched and delicious. This may have contributed to our dear preacher becoming diabetic, or it may not. The details of his diet were not my business and how he and his wife were

65

handling the situation was not information I needed to know but, of course, I always worried that one day we would need a preacher for our beloved preacher.

We received news that our preacher had been hospitalized and was going in for some kind of surgery, we hoped with fingers crossed and not knowing all of the details, that he would make it out to offer another sermon.

Then, one sunny afternoon some coworkers and I were sitting in the office at the mortuary, it was some weeks after the news of the clergy man's hospitalization, when in walks the preacher himself! He was wearing one of his famous multi-colored bow ties and smile that we had all come to adore. On one foot he wore a big black medical boot over a tight wrapping of gauze. After some hugs and asking about his well-being, then joking about his hospital stay, he informed us that he had lost a toe. They had to amputate it due to the damage caused by his diabetes. He plopped himself down in a chair at the arrangement table and just like a family who had lost a loved one he said "I have lost my toe, I would like to arrange his funeral. Just a small affair, nothing fancy, maybe a couple of people could speak" and then he stated that he would need a funeral director to officiate. He chuckled at his

Speaking of the dead by Chelsea L. Tolman

joke and we laughed with him and made the most appropriate jokes, as you can imagine.

He didn't actually have the toe to memorialize, we just said a few solemn words there in the office and giggled, but if we had had the toe, I assure you that it would have been buried properly, like any human appendage deserves.

Speaking of the dead by Chelsea L. Tolman

THE EAR

There comes a time in every young embalmers life when they get to reconstruct part of a person in real life, not just on plastic skulls in college. To explain, when I was in school we had a class called Restorative Art. We were to reconstruct an entire face out of clay on a plastic skull. Start with the nose and move out from there. You are not judged on how good your clay face looks aesthetically but how accurate the dimensions are. There are staunch rules regarding the placement of facial features, like, your face is made up of three equal parts; the top of your forehead to the line of your eyebrows is the same distance as the top of your eyebrows to the bottom of your nose and then subsequently, the bottom of your nose to the bottom of your chin is the same distance as the other two measurements. There are tons of these rules of proportions and we must know them all. In reconstruction if you know the proportions of one part of the face you can reasonably determine the proportions of another structure that you are trying to recreate.

I will always remember my first. We got a man who had shot himself, resulting in a mangled ear. It was beyond repair and it was the ear on the "the viewing side" (industry jargon for the right side of the face, which is the side that faces that the family and friends view from) My boss at the time was distressed, we had a lot of other work to do and this reconstruction would take a lot of time. I was of course ecstatic, not that the man had shot himself but that I now had the opportunity to build an ear from scratch and put my training to the test. I pled my case about needing the experience and that I would have to do these things for real at some point anyway.

Finally, I was given the go ahead to fix the ear on my own. So, like any artist I pulled out my supplies and spread them out next to me. Waxes, chemicals and cosmetics. Once organized and settled, I sat in a chair next to my patient and turned on some tunes for inspiration. Using the wax, a chemical cauterizing agent, ligature, and cosmetics, I tried and failed and tried another way more than once. I do not remember how long it took me. I know I was careful and precise and referenced the other ear until I had created an ear that was suitable for viewing. Totally proud of myself.

I was then given the honor of walking the family in to see the man for the first time. They were nervous, not knowing what they were going to see. I was nervous that they would be pleased with my work. I will never forget the relief on the family members faces when they saw their loved one with two perfectly placed ears.

IS IT REALLY THAT GROSS?

It is inevitable that when people find out what I do for a living the subject of "gross" comes up. I can honestly say that I have always found the workings of living things to be incredibly interesting. As a child I played with insects, well, not so much played with them as dissected them. I was a master at catching bugs. Grasshoppers, spiders, slugs and snails, I had an array of all of these things in my back-yard tree house. It wasn't a tree house that was in a tree, it was two wooden boxes that sat in the grass on a top of a low hill in our backyard. There were windows and a door and on occasion my dad would stack them on top of each other making it two stories and attached a fireman's pole to slide down from the top level. They had a shelf that ran along each side of the interior walls and this is where I kept my bugs in jars. The entire shelf lined with mason jars holding various bugs both living and dead. It was my place.

I would cut the insects open, cook them, boil them and anything else I could think of doing to discover how those little parts worked and what they looked like. No matter what I tried though, I always got mush, the parts being too small for me to see anything clearly. Yet I continued to explore in my backyard butcher shop. Please do not worry about all of those poor insects that I experimented on, I didn't mean any harm. In fact, I took to breeding them. My childhood logic was that I was replacing the ones that I had destroyed with fresh new lives. I could not in good conscience take from the world an insect life without finding a way to give it back. This was, of course, a kid's way of thinking about how the world worked. And just because you are wondering, no, I never experimented on anything bigger than insects.

That being said, the fascination of being a mortician included the interest in the human body and all of its parts, especially since there isn't much that can "gross" me out, most of the time. Not long after I started college I decided that a good way to see all the parts of a human was to head to the medical examiner's office (ME's office for short) where they performed autopsies. Here they purposefully cut into flesh and organs to discover the mystery of why the person died. I decided that at the ME's office was where I was sure to convince someone to let me see the insides of a human body in a place where they had to take them apart anyway. After some negotiating, I was able to set up tours for my college class. Once a week we would be able to watch from behind a glass wall, a real live autopsy! I announced to the class the details and to come see me to sign up. Some did, most did not.

After a few weeks of our group religiously showing up to watch the autopsies through a glass window we were told that we could enter the room and witness, up close and personal, the things that make us breathe and walk and talk and move about. The caveat being we had to bring our own gear (smocks, shoe covers, gloves and masks). For those of us who joined, it was a mad dash to the school and the mortuaries we worked at, begging for supplies so that we could be part of this experience.

We showed up the next scheduled tour day. The lobby of the ME's office was decorated in 1960's style colors and patterns. And scattered about the carpeted floor were glass boxes holding various medical anomalies with a plaque describing what each box held. We walked around patiently waiting for someone to come get us and direct us to the autopsy room while holding in our hands the precious equipment we had all acquired for this day. A young girl finally showed up and asked if we had our gear and like toddlers showing the teacher how well they did at following instructions we held up our smocks and shoe covers proving we had completed this assignment. She turned around and told us to follow her.

We entered the room with the glass wall that we had been standing in for the previous visits, here she stopped and instructed us to put on our gear before we walked through a side door that entered the autopsy room. We helped each other tie smock strings and made sure shoes were fully covered. We had also brought a jar of Vicks vapor rub and smeared a dab under our noses (we were warned that the smell was going to be intolerable and Vicks is what they used to obscure the odor). Once we pulled on our gloves, we were finally granted access.

As we walked into the room bathed in bright fluorescent lighting and shockingly white walls and floor, there were portable tables everywhere, each held a body in all sorts of conditions and states of dress. The Medical Examiner greeted us all and showed us around. We met the photographer who was standing on a ladder hunched over a body, taking pictures for the file. We passed by a man burnt so badly that all that was left of him was a blackened head and torso, other bodies with tragic stories surrounded us on all sides.

Speaking of the dead by Chelsea L. Tolman

It was overwhelming. I wanted to see all of them, I wanted to study each one and look at the wounds and I had so many questions! But, we were being led on a tour, so I followed the Medical Examiner to where he stopped at a table on our right which beheld an older gentleman, the back of his head directed towards us. He explained that the man had supposedly shot himself with a shot gun, the entrance wound was inside his mouth and there was no exit wound. He also told us that he questioned the suicide only because it was rare for an elderly person to commit suicide plus to accomplish this the man would have had to pull the trigger with his toe, a difficult feat for a younger, limber person made even more difficult for an elderly man with arthritis. He then told us that he chose to bring us to this gentleman first because they were about to start the autopsy and he wanted us to see what a shotgun did to brain tissue. He instructed a Diener (a morgue worker who helps the ME) to make the cut as we watched. As the scalp came open there were pieces of the skull that had to be pulled away, having been shattered by the blast and as that happened, the substance that was left was like oatmeal. It was incredible. The ME took a piece of this and showed us the trails that the shotgun had left after bouncing around inside

75

the skull. That was my first experience with an autopsy. And there were more after that.

Muscles, tendons, organs, tissue, and the smells! It was all there. There were two incredible moments for me that I will never forget. One was holding an intact human brain, I held it in my hands! In awe I cradled this solid mass of gray matter in my hands and reveled at this thing that is responsible for our thoughts and movement of muscle and experiencing emotions. It was incredible to imagine this bulk of tissue that I held was the same thing that gave me awe that I actually held it! The second was holding a human heart, I touched with my fingers the very organ that is in charge of the circulation of lifegiving blood through our bodies. Without it we could not function as a human. In these moments there was nothing I wanted more than to experience this. In all of the time I spent at the ME's office I saw the aftermath of car accidents, fires, stabbings, gunshots, bodies left in the elements for days and more. And it was so cool!

And it was humbling. There is so much tragedy for the families who have lost someone to these calamities. What must they be going through? Did they know that there loved one was laying on a table at the ME's office scattered amongst other tables with other loved ones lying on them? The most tragic were the bodies that I knew the family would never get to see again, because they were too damaged by whatever accident befell them for any type of viewing. The horrific things that happened to these very real people is tragic and sad. I do not revel in the casualties of death in any way. I understand and feel the pain and grief of those who have experienced these losses. These things are real, and I am sorry for their families. My captivation is seeing the lumps and forms and strings that make up ourselves. It is enthralling to me to see and touch the fibers of muscles, globs of fats and all the layers of the skin that make us these complicated creatures called humans.

However, with all the manners of death there can be that give me and other curious people out there like me the ability to see inside our incredible bags of bones and tissue, is it really that gross?

SILENT CEMETERY

Some funeral directors make it a habit of watching the news before beginning the day. Sometimes we find it a good indicator of what the day had in store for us. Sadly, we are looking for the shootings, accidents, fires or any disaster that may mean "work" in the funeral business. On this particular day, I had had a long night and awoke the next morning in a rush, taking no notice of the day's headlines. I was only focused on getting to work and looking professional and refreshed.

Apparently, during the night a man had robbed a convenience store and shot and killed the clerk who worked there, then he was able to run away before the police could arrive. After some detective work, the police were able to track down who he was and where he lived. The SWAT team surrounded his house and his confused and elderly mother opened the front door. She tried to get answers from the men in black gear, carrying shields and guns. Instead, they pushed her out of the way and entered the house just as her son was coming out of a back room brandishing a gun, as he turned his weapon on the police, they shot him before he could fire. Tragically, he died there, in his living room, in front of his mother. The man was in his forties, he had a drug problem and his mother was the ever-nurturing kind. I was told she kept telling the police "He was a good boy". We got the call later that day to come and pick up his body.

We laid the man down on the embalming table and looked over the wounds. He was riddled with bullet holes. He was not autopsied, yet, his body was still a mess. All we could think of was what his poor mother was going through after watching this happen to her son.

When the family came in to make arrangements, it was determined that there would be a small graveside, no obituary was to be published and no one was to know when the service was to take place. The family religion was Baha'i which meant a traditional shrouding with prayers and rose water. Local Baha'i clergy refused perform the ritual and none of the family members wanted to do it, no one even wanted to see his body. This meant the funeral home was to perform the shrouding.

We were given instructions by the church on how the shroud was to be wrapped and a sheet detailing the prayers to be said. We had no idea what we were doing. The family dropped off the shroud and the rose water and a coworker and I took all of these supplies and headed to the prep room to start the task. The table the man lay on was in the center of the room, ringed on two sides with white cabinets and cream counter-tops. The back end of the room was slightly dimmed where open shelves of towels and chemicals sat. The rest of the room was covered in bright fluorescent lighting, making the room feel much more cheerful than the situation called for. We laid out all of the instructions given to us. We sutured the man's wounds to prevent them from seeping through the shroud and washed and dried the body. The shroud came in strips and the strips were to be wrapped in a specific way and the rose water was to be sprinkled at certain points of the shrouding. It turned out to be a relaxing experience, wrapping, sprinkling, saying the prayers. Once we finished, we placed the shrouded man in his casket and closed the lid. Giving us our own kind of closure to the experience.

The day of the graveside was bitterly cold, the grass and trees were covered in ice and frost. We loaded the casket into the hearse, grabbed all of the supplies we needed, tissues, blankets etc. and drove to the gravesite. We wanted to make sure that everything was set up and ready by the time the family arrived. We laid out the carefully folded blankets and placed tissue packets on the chairs. My staff and I then pulled the casket out of the back of the hearse and walked through the crunchy, frozen grass to place it over the open grave, its final destination.

The family arrived all at once bundled in black coats and scarves. When anyone spoke, it was in hushed tones

Speaking of the dead by Chelsea L. Tolman

giving a reverent silence to the air. I watched the scene as the handful of family members took their seats in front of the simple wooden casket, bare of any adornments or flowers. Stretched out on all sides were the silent graves of others, huge trees covered in ice stood as watchmen over their dead. The grass was frosted with white aside from the trails marking where people had walked over from the street, and ominous grey clouds hovered in the sky above. There was no color other than the green of the tent and chair covers. The clergy stood at the head of the casket and I took my place at the back of the tent to watch and listen and reflect on what this family was going through. Why did this man do what he did? What drives someone to the desperation of killing another person? As the clergy spoke, his voice reverberated off the trees and yet seemed strangely muted as the freezing rain started again adding quiet tinkles of tiny ice droplets hitting the already frozen landscape.

When the service was over, no one spoke, the family got up, walked to their cars and simply drove away. I waited at the grave until the vault lid was closed, then got into the hearse and drove back to the mortuary. Once back, I noticed the tingling in my fingers and toes as they defrosted from the time I was standing in the freezing cold. I was so wrapped up in the experience that I did not notice how I was close to losing limbs to frostbite. As I thawed, I considered what this family was experiencing. Their son, brother, friend was dead, yet it was the brutal death of a man who brutally murdered another man. The silence of the cemetery and the colorless backdrop seemed fitting for laying this man to rest. I hope the family has found some peace, I hope the dead man has found some peace. I will always remember this experience and how the choices we make directly affect the people closest to us.

Speaking of the dead by Chelsea L. Tolman

DRAWING THE LINE

Any person who works in the service industry has the challenge of balancing a healthy work and home life. When responsible for assisting other people in the depth of deep emotions it will eventually get to you, nobody is immune. My mother is a social worker and she and I have very similar experiences of broken people with heart wrenching stories. We have talked at length on how to deal with it. Usually I deal with this sorrow by reasoning that this is not my grief, the death didn't happen to me, I never knew this person, so I cannot feel their loss. Unfortunately, this doesn't really work.

While sitting in a room full of people that are in the full swing of grief and they are all handling it differently, it becomes my grief. Not the loss of course but the empathy attached to it. One person is angry, another quiet and stoic, while two more are actively sobbing through the motions. It is a balance every minute. I pay attention to every person and how I acknowledge that they lost someone they love. Moving from a soft demeanor to address one person and then turning to the pragmatist and get down to business, then taking a moment with the silent and make sure that their wishes are being heard. It is a rush for me to balance and move and delegate tasks for all of those involved. I do thrive on the details, yet, even I can only take so much of it.

The funeral industry is demanding, I'll get home to finally relax only to get a call minutes later from a family member in a panic because she forgot to include someone in an obituary (already published), or mom found the pants her husband was supposed to buried in tomorrow and asks, "Is it too late?" Even though he has already been dressed and viewed. It has been a while since I have been on call at night on a regular basis, but I do remember the dinners I had to walk out of or family events I had to leave from to go receive a person from their home or a hospital or care facility.

We, as an industry put home on hold to make sure the grieving families are taken care of and the deceased bodies are cared for. It is a strong person indeed to marry a mortician. For most of my mortician life it has been all about the families, with me stating that they needed me more than my own family. "Leave the work at work and the home at home", that is a rule and that works most of the time. Unfortunately, we do forget and life travels in its own way to push or pull your heart and mind in directions you are actively trying to avoid. This can be said for other professions as well. We are human and our sense of sensibility gets distorted after a while and exhaustion kicks in. So, where do you draw the line?

The answer is different for everybody, funeral directors need vacations and time off. I remember when I decided to stop going on night calls. I felt a bit liberated that I didn't have to have my phone within arm's reach at all times. I also felt a little shameful that I was possibly letting someone down, whether it was family or a coworker. After thirteen years of constantly being on call, on the ball, 2:00am wake ups to drive to whatever home in the backwoods of the country, the hospital morgue, or the nursing home, it was a little bit hard to let go.

I have the perfect example of where to draw the line. I met with the family of a woman who had some deep-seeded anger for each other. Even before I had met this family face-to-face I was given a recount from the team who had picked the woman up from the hospital. There was a daughter present when they arrived. She acted like the sole guardian for her mother and had demanded that she be let into the back of the transport van to ride next her mother's body to the mortuary. The team explained to her that this was not possible due to the lack of seats and seatbelts, but she was welcome to follow them back in her own car to ensure that her mother reached the funeral home unharmed. Once they reached the funeral home the woman then demanded she be let inside the building to sit with her mother throughout the night. The team explained that they were to perform the embalming right then and that the daughter would most certainly not want to be present for that, thankfully, she agreed. The solution was that once the funeral home opened the next morning she should call and find out who the funeral director would be and then make arrangements with them to sit with her mother's body just as she requested. I was that funeral director.

It was not long after opening hours that I started to receive phone calls from the family. I was given demands that so and so was not to see or touch the woman's body and there were claims that so and so has no authority to make decisions regarding the woman who was dead. It was insane! I wrote down names and their relations and the demands given, trying to keep it all straight. After many conversations it became clear that nothing was clear. The reality was that each party was headed by children of the deceased and each party had just as much right as the other to make arrangements, as long as they all mostly agreed with each other.

Speaking of the dead by Chelsea L. Tolman

I explained that it was best for all of the children to come in and talk out what was going to happen to their mother. Unfortunately, neither side was willing to be in the same room as the other. So, to get a grip on situation, I made two appointments and met with each party separately.

I have met with warring family members before. I have sat in a room and witnessed arguments, fighting, crying and anger but this situation made me physically ill. A woman was dead. She was lying in a room in the back of the funeral home and her children were making the most unbelievable claims about what their siblings did or did not do to her. I will not recount what I was told in these meetings, but I will never forget the images they created for me. In all my years as a mortician I have never met with a more dysfunctional family than this one.

One daughter in particular headed her brigade with brute force. Many times I had to explain what her and her siblings rights were and that the only way her mother was going to be buried or cremated was with some kind of agreement with her siblings and someone had to pay the bill. Most states require two thirds of the children to agree on disposition (mainly for cremation), the firm I worked for required all of the children's signatures and in this case I was totally grateful for that. With all of the claims, demands and fighting there was one daughter who made everything ten times harder than it should have been

I learned from this daughter, who had already spent hours of my time with demands, who now dismissed the fact that it was Sunday and the mortuary was closed and that I was having a family event that her need to see her mother, again, was more important at that moment than anything else and personal time.

Care for the caregiver. Self-care is a difficult thing when there are people out there who need help. Take it from me, you are much more likely to help others when you learn to draw the line.

Speaking of the dead by Chelsea L. Tolman

STANDING OVATION

It is not common to receive a standing ovation for simply doing your job. In fact, it is not something I have ever heard anyone say has happened during the day-to-day tasks we are assigned. It usually takes doing something extraordinary like giving a presentation or winning an award type of things, unless you're me. That may sound like I'm bragging, but that is only because I am. I have never heard of anyone else being applauded by a group of nurses in the middle of the night, simply because I did my job, on my own, without help, but there ya have it, it happened and now I am most definitely bragging about it.

It was a late night. I do not remember what time I received the call, but the deceased was located a hospital which meant that I was going on my own without a second partner (this was procedure at this firm). Sleepy and tired, I dragged my cot to the required floor and started looking for room numbers and the nurses station located closest to it. It is standard procedure that before you go carting off deceased bodies you let someone in the hospital know you are doing it and sign something that says you did it. We can't have people just running off with dead bodies without a paper trail. I found

Speaking of the dead by Chelsea L. Tolman

a nurse behind a desk ticking away at her computer, focused on her work. Hospitals at night are strangely quiet. It's not like during the day with blaring lights, a hustle and bustle of people with flowers and balloons or hospital beds carrying patients for tests or surgeries. The hallways are dark, people are sleeping, the only noises are the beeps and clicks of monitors and occasional whir of oxygen tanks, or the soft voices of staff gossiping about the day crew.

I parked my cot against the hallway wall and walked to the desk of the still working nurse. She looked up at me as I approached, her concentrated brow turned to one of friendliness and smiles and she asked, "How may I help you?" I explained that I was with the mortuary to receive so and so who had passed away. Kind and helpful she pulled out the paperwork, verified the room number and pointed me in the direction I needed to go. I turned and walked towards to my cot when I heard from behind me "Where is your partner?" I turned and answered "I am here by myself". Silence. And then she stated "Oh, well I can't help you right now." With a new furrow replacing the friendly one from before. I have been given this speech before, that mortuaries cannot expect the hospital staff to be at their beck and call at all hours of the night. I was getting used to this resistance from people. I will

Speaking of the dead by Chelsea L. Tolman

admit that being a small female has its limitations. But after some time working in this field, constantly having to prove myself, I had a bag of tricks to do what was needed and it didn't hurt that I was wickedly strong back in those days. I returned her comment with "I got this, I don't need any help."

Incredulity crossed her face, questions ran silently through her gaze at me and I whisked my cot away to the room that held my charge before she could argue. I did my job. I raised the hospital bed up to be just a little higher than my cot, scrunched the sheet as far as I could under the deceased and rolled the body towards me to grab the ends from the other side, wrapping him up like a burrito. I now had the edges of the sheet facing me and simply pulled the sheet and person onto my cot, all by myself, just like a dozen times before. I made my way back to the hall and surely a waiting nurse. As I approached the desk, to my surprise, there were 5-6 people gathered at the nurse's station, all standing, probably waiting for me to come out and ask for help. A sweet and glowing smile spread across the nurses' face as I walked up with my cot with the body of the deceased secured. "Wow, that is what I call girl power!" She exclaimed, "We have never had a woman come here by herself!" "You go girl!" Then they all started applauding, quietly mind you so as not to wake the patients, but they were all standing and applauding me so I'll take it! It may be a little thing to some of you, yet in that time, in that area, it was unheard of. Yep, I will brag about that.

Speaking of the dead by Chelsea L. Tolman

LOST SOLE

In most cases, once a grave is dug, the vault company mounts what we call a "lowering device" over the open hole, this is a metal tubing structure placed around the edges of the grave. The frame straddles the opening on all sides and has thick straps that cross the center. It is custom that the pall bearers, either six or eight people, carry the casket over the lowering device to then set it down on the center straps and there it sits, safe and secure, until it's time to lower it all the way down to the bottom.

This day I was the funeral director in charge. The cemetery was located outside of the city, which was a fairly long drive from the mortuary. It was arranged that we would meet the family at the grave instead of driving in procession the entire way. This was a small-town cemetery, sitting in the foothills of a low desert mountain with buildings and houses of the tiny town scattered about in the valley below. The cemetery, as well as the town, was all dirt and dust and it was blazing hot that day. My coworker and I had arrived early to get things set up, we unloaded the flowers and placed them around the grave, giving sharp bursts of color and life to the otherwise dusty, careworn atmosphere. We put mints and tissues on the folding chairs, set up the register book for guests to sign and then we waited.

To pass the time we walked around the cemetery looking at the graves, trying to find the oldest ones. The graves were simple but clearly loved, as evidenced by the decor. The flowers were mostly silk, standing in vases or lovingly placed near a headstone and were in various stages of fading and fraying due to the dry scratchy desert. Dusty trinkets of plastic angels and frogs, wind chimes and rocks with inspirational sayings lovingly placed to identify the personalities of those lying below. The most recent graves were mounded with dirt to account for settling in the months to come and marked with simple plastic placards until the headstones could be ordered and placed. We talked about the unassuming air of the cemetery and discussed certain headstones that caught our eye, then we sat under the awning provided for the family to escape the blistering sun.

By the time the guests started arriving we had already spent 45 minutes baking in the heat. As people walked up they brought more flowers to set around and we added them to the ones already placed, enjoying the added color. Some of the guests started walking around looking for family members graves who had been buried in years past, telling stories of grandma so and so, or uncle big shot or how many days baby Jane had lived, or they simply stood under the awning looking for relief from the scorching sun.

We soon got word that some of the family had gotten lost along the way, including the bulk of the pall bearers. It had been so long since they had visited that they had forgotten a crucial turn-off and were thirty minutes in the wrong direction before they realized the error, so, we all hunkered down and coped with the heat as best we could. Some of the guests stripped off suit jackets, the ladies sat on the chairs and peeled off heeled footwear that were impractical for any cemetery let alone this dry dirt laden place. There was a cooler with cold water provided by the vault company, but unfortunately not enough for everybody, so the staff and I let the guests have it all as we smiled and internally cringed from tickles of sweat dripping under our black suits, all the while trying to look refreshed and professional and avoiding the urge to snap at every grieving person who, legitimately, had it worse than we did. The reward for our best behavior was that, when this was all over, we could strip off our jackets, get some food and much needed water before the hour and a half drive back to the mortuary.

Speaking of the dead by Chelsea L. Tolman

After what seemed like an hour, the lost cars did arrive. Even though I was irritable and ready to be done with this day, I gave the family time to greet each other, I let them talk a bit and shake off the adrenaline of being lost and late. Then finally, it was time to get started with the funeral. Thankfully the grave was located close to the road, meaning we didn't have to carry the casket very far. The pall bearers met me at the back of the hearse to collect the casket bearing the guest of honor. I gave the pall bearers detailed instructions; grab the handles as the casket is pulled out, turn slowly to head in the correct direction, walk together until the casket is centered over the grave and set it down gently. I also gave a few safety warnings. We had the challenge of eight pall bearers which meant they must take smaller strides to avoid walking on each other's heels, the dry dirt was uneven and rocky so higher steps were advised and of course we faced the added sweat factor, which meant, if hands became slippery, we could set the casket down and start over. These are standard instructions that I had given many times before. However, I never thought to warn them of the impending doom about to befall the funeral director, me.

Carefully and as instructed, the pallbearers got their grip on the handles, made the turn and we started our short walk. I took my place at the end of the casket that was to go over the lowering device first so that I could guide and give instructions as needed. Then, suddenly, on the final steps of approaching the lowering device, my shoe caught on something! To this day I am not sure what it caught on, but it was caught tightly. Imagine, the casket and all eight men, in full motion at this point, carrying the heavy casket straight towards me doing so quickly. I still had a hold of my end of the casket. I looked at the gentleman closest to me, with what I imagine to be a look of horror, and mouthed, "Stop!!" Of course, the plan was in motion already and there was no way to slow the momentum of these men, so, I wrenched my foot as hard as I could and barely got out of the way before I ended in the grave myself. The casket was placed successfully, and I was still upright. Even with the adrenaline still rushing through me from the near mishap, I started my way to the microphone to begin the service when I realized that one foot was walking on solid ground. Seriously! I slowly looked down at my feet only to find that the entire sole of one shoe was gone, just gone! The only thing I had left on my foot was the flappy leather top of my shoe. Not wanting to draw attention to myself I slowly walked around the grave, hoping beyond hope that the sole of my shoe was left outside of the grave and not in it. Luckily, I found it. The thick black sole of my funeral shoe was lying on the ground right where it had caught but I still couldn't tell what had happened. Red cheeked, I am sure, I stooped down as nonchalantly as possible, grabbed the rubber sole and hobbled, with what pride I could muster and with what I hoped to be grace, to the hearse and I chucked the damn betraying sole right into the opened passenger window. I gathered what little patience I could still muster and shuffled back to the microphone to start the funeral service that was slated to last thirty minutes, hoping that no one had noticed my near demise turned wardrobe malfunction.

Of course, I conducted myself like a professional despite my internal desire to scream. Since I was conducting, I had put together some stories and poetry that reflected what the family had shared with me about the woman lying in the casket. Once I was finished, it was time for an open mic (where people in the crowd are invited to get and speak) and even though I instructed the crowd to walk over to me to talk into the microphone most thought it was better to stay under the tent, which meant that I had to deliver the microphone to wherever that person was standing. I walked with one foot in a proper shoe and one foot using my toes trying to move lightly and gracefully like a gazelle so that no one would detect my new irksome swagger. When the service finally ended, I made my way to the road and leaned against the hearse and tried to shake off the frustration of all that had happened. To my relief, it seemed that no one caught the mishap or they were too kind to bring attention to my embarrassment. The guests were milling around and visiting with each other, still looking for the graves of other family members and talking about which favorite restaurant they would meet at for dinner. Then, I was approached by a woman, she slowly looked around us as if to assure that no one else was within earshot before politely asking me if I was okay. She had seen the whole thing! We talked and chuckled about my near demise and commented about how far we were from help had an accident occurred, which would have resulted in difficulty getting medical care. It lifted my spirits to have a comrade in the bizarre event that had befallen me.

Finally, after what seemed like another hour, the family dispersed and left the cemetery and we were free to leave. We said goodbye to the cemetery crew who were waiting to lower the casket. We got in the hearse and drove away from that place. Of course, we were now due for a meal and I with only one and a half shoes. Once we arrived at the restaurant, I gathered my pride once again and "gracefully" made my entrance into the restaurant and once we ate I shuffled to the exit to at last get back in the hearse and go the hell home!

99

Speaking of the dead by Chelsea L. Tolman

Speaking of the dead by Chelsea L. Tolman

ANGRY

During my morning ritual of walking into the embalming room familiarizing myself with the dead who had been brought in during the night, I was hit by a feeling of what I can only describe as trouble. It was a palpable feeling, like something drifting through the air and it felt like it was coming from a man lying on a table nearest the entrance door. I would have guessed him to be in his late sixties. He had a head full of salt and pepper hair, combed straight back and over his ears. He had a full beard and mustache neatly groomed and somehow, he looked angry. He had a tight expression, his eyes seemed strained and his lips were pursed. Laying at his feet were the clothes he would be dressed in for his funeral, overalls and a green and plaid long-sleeved shirt. I was taken back a bit by the overwhelming feeling that I should just leave him alone. So, I looked him over and read his toe tag but did not pat his head or arm like I normally would with our newly attained guests, I felt that he would not welcome the gesture.

On occasion my coworkers at this firm would pretend to leave for the day and then when they knew I was cleaning the building, alone, with the darkness closing around the building, they would sneak back in through a rear door and turn off lights, or turn them on, move things that I had already put away or open and close doors. I never knew if I was just really tired or if these jokers were hiding about, trying to scare me.

One night as I was cleaning the building after a late-night visitation. I had just started vacuuming the main hallway. It was covered in dark carpet and was long and wide and down each side was a series of doors that led to the viewing rooms. As I began vacuuming at one end of the hallway, I thought I heard a shout. I stopped for a second, dismissed it as the sound of the vacuum and continued. Then I heard the shout again, it sounded like "Stop it!" So, I turned the vacuum off and called out "Hello?" Silence. I called out again," Hello, is somebody there?" Nothing. It had been a long day, I was tired, and wanted to go home, so I turned the vacuum back on, only to again here "Stop it!" Only this time there was a little more force behind the words. Now irritated, I turned off the vacuum, again, and went to search the building while calling out "Who's there?" I checked all of the rooms, walked through the back hallways, I turned on all the lights to see if I catch a coworker hiding in a corner, but only found empty rooms and silence. I just wanted to finish my chores and go home, and I was getting angry.

As I walked into the embalming room, there was the man I had seen earlier. I don't know if he was ever angry in life, but he definitely had a feeling around him that was harsh. I asked him if he had yelled at me and when he didn't answer, I giggled at myself for expecting a dead man to talk. I turned off the light and left the room.

As I walked back through the hallways to continue my tasks, some of the lights I know I had previously turned on were now off. This made me think for sure that it was my coworkers, so I started calling their cell phones to see if I could hear ringing from a corner and catch my joker. Everyone I called answered their phone, there was no one else was in the building. Baffled and irritated, I went back to my vacuum and turned the switch on, then as clear as ever I heard "Stop it!", the voice sounded as if the person was standing right in front of me! That was it, I was done, this was too weird. I left the vacuum where it was, turned off all the lights and made my way out of the building. On my way out, I spoke to the angry man again. I told him to rest in peace but guaranteed him that I would be back in the morning to finish the rest of the vacuuming and he would just have to deal with it! And if it was him. He was not the only one who was angry that night!

CHRISTMAS CONTROVERSY

I was managing a small funeral home in a small town and had already held several events at my location, fundraisers, local art receptions, car shows, civil servant's luncheons and more. Now I was determined to have a Christmas memorial service. This meant I would hold a service that focused on celebrating all of the lives of the deceased people we had served during that year.

I was warned by my coworkers that to decorate was one thing, but people would not come to the funeral home during a time of year meant for joy and happiness to be part of a memorial service, "It's too hard" they said, "People are busy during this time" they said, "No one wants to go to the funeral home for Christmas".

The town was all about Christmas. There was big parade that stomped through the town and all the local businesses had a float or car or donated people to hand out candy canes. I chose to have the funeral home staff drive our van in the parade and throw out candy to the crowd. My staff and I decorated a Christmas tree and placed it in the lobby of the funeral home. Garland hung from the fireplace mantel, wreaths adorned the front doors and it truly felt like a funeral

105

home for the holidays. So, I planned a Christmas memorial service. Despite the warnings.

It was to be held in the chapel of the funeral home and the whole town would be invited. My staff busied ourselves by distributing fliers to local businesses and mailed out invitations to everyone in our files. Then together we spent hours in my home hand making wooden ornaments adorning the name of each and every person the funeral home had buried or cremated that year and hung them on the Christmas tree in the lobby. I was excited but a little nervous that my coworkers would be right, and no one would show up.

On the day of the service I set out the food and drinks. Pastries with raspberry filling, cucumber sandwiches, cookies, spiced cider and hot chocolate. The food table was placed in the largest viewing room right down the center. The table cloths were a cheery red and I had centerpieces made from a local florist with holly and poinsettias. It was an evening service and already darkening outside. With the fireplace roaring and all of the lights on, everything was ready and it was a holiday funeral home for sure.

Guests began arriving dressed in their Christmas finery and entered the viewing room to get a drink or handheld yummy. Then as more people showed up they mingled and

Speaking of the dead by Chelsea L. Tolman

talked with their drinks and plates in hand. Soon the funeral home was buzzing with people. I remember looking around at all the faces of the families that I had previously served, knowing that I had made the right decision by not taking my coworkers advice. Everything was working out just as I had planned.

It was going to be a wonderful program. I had invited several speakers including local clergy of different religions. I hired a very talented singer and had my own speech prepared. The speakers sat in the chairs at the front of the chapel and the musicians took their places. Everyone was there, and everything was ready. My staff and I ushered the guests into the chapel and quickly had every seat filled, it was a full house!

I officiated and introduced all of the speakers in turn. Each message was full and heartfelt, the music was perfectly performed. There was some laughter and some tears as each part of the program took place. During one of the songs my staff and I snuck out to the lobby and took the ornaments off of the tree and placed them in a box, a surprise for guests at the end of the program.

When the last song was over, my staff and I took the box and stood at the front of the chapel. I gave a speech about the honor of serving those who died throughout the year and instructed the families who were there that when their loved ones name was called to stand and collect their ornament to take home and place on their own tree.

As I called out each name and the family members stood, I remembered the death, I remembered the service and remembered the grieving of that family. I hugged them all and loved that I could do this little thing for them.

Holidays are especially difficult when you ache for a loved one to be there yet, they are gone. So many people thanked us all for putting this thing together and for not forgetting them during the holidays. It was truly heartwarming to have the opportunity to serve them again.

REGRET AND GRIEF

One day a gentleman walked through the door of the mortuary. He was expertly dressed in a high-end suit and tie. His shoes were clearly made of real leather and polished to a high sheen. He sported short, dark hair which was spiked on top, undoubtedly styled by a barber in a fancy shop where your cut comes with a clean shave and a warm towel. These were things that we were not used to in our small country town. He was impressive as he walked into our office with his resume in hand. He enchanted us all with his beautiful toothfull smile and natural charisma, his charm could rival any salesman. I think we hired him on the spot, if only for the sheer ambition he exuded and dared us to test.

Sometimes people just click the moment they meet. If you have ever felt this, then you know. It is a strange, immediate feeling of familiarity like you had known each other well before that moment. That is what happened to me the day he walked through the door and I knew we were destined to be best friends. The mortuary was not necessarily looking for another employee. We did okay, sometimes the days and nights got hectic and strenuous but overall, we had enough downtime to get small hours of much-needed respite.

Speaking of the dead by Chelsea L. Tolman

We even had the occasion to tend to a little vegetable garden at the back of our red brick building. But he walked in the door and we found ourselves with a new set of helping hands.

He and I hit it off like two teenage girls. We loved the same 80s music and old black and white movies. On his first day of working with me, as we were running errands, we stopped at a convenience store for a coke. The bins at the check-out counter held colorful braided hemp bracelets. The ones that promised to last a lifetime. We never said a word, we both saw them, we gave a knowing look to each other and I said the cashier "We'll take two of those". We ran to the car and placed them on our ankles, swearing to each other that we would never take them off as long as we were friends.

As I taught him the ropes of the funeral trade, he loved and absorbed all of it. He took to funeral service like a moth to a flame. At least the service part, the embalming room presented challenges for my new-found friend. The reality that our beings could produce so many unpleasant noises, fluids, and smells made for a test in his seemingly unbreakable resolve. Many times I excitedly called him to the back room yelling "You have got to see this!", and then chuckle as he ran for the exit when he couldn't handle what I wanted to show him. He soon learned to approach my call with caution, carefully poking his head through the door, cracking one eye open just enough to look like Jack Nicholson in "The Shining," only he was the one who was afraid and I saying, "Here's Johnny"! Through squinted eyes he would peer through the doorway at me ready to look away quickly in case I was trying to show him something that I was fascinated about, meaning he would not be.

His skill in meeting and talking to people completely made up for his lack of ability to embrace the back rooms. He had an attention for detail and a flare for decorating with pictures and flowers that astounded the men and women he served. Every visitation room was a show, the family memorabilia he placed so skillfully you would have thought that you were walking through a movie set, or a model home. The flower arrangements that came in for the deceased were always positioned according to height and color for the perfect balance to accent the casket and the person lying inside of it. He made friends with everyone he met and many times I would talk about a family that we had previously served and he would give me the update on how they were doing, offer their phone number and say we should stop by their house for a visit. I was quickly learning that this man was a social butterfly of epic proportions. He knew people from all over the world and he was never without his phone which was constantly buzzing or ringing with messages or calls from

Speaking of the dead by Chelsea L. Tolman

Dave or Brian or Celeste, any number of names I could list here certain he knew someone who possessed it. His cell phone was his life and was either on his hip or in his hand.

Our friendship moved outside of work and I eventually met his boyfriend and neighbors. We had barbeques and parties and spent many late nights sitting around a fire roasting some type of meat and toasting to each other's accomplishments. These evenings usually ending in deep conversation or dancing on the porch. Eventually I ended up moving into the house directly across from the boys, making an even more intimate bond for everyone involved. Our friendship deepened and over the years we had accumulated so many memories, lived through tragic circumstances and celebrated holidays, birthdays and ordinary days. He was the man on the riding lawnmower waving to passersby in expensive cargo shorts, designer shirts and a wide brimmed bonnet that would make any decent southern woman jealous. He won awards with his Tupperware parties and could refinish a wooden counter-top like a professional. We were besties in the sense that besties are with the added bonus that to spend a day together was as easy as walking across the street. And like all good things, these things had to end.

He struggled with balancing a party life mixed with a work life. He struggled with his health. He struggled with his relationship. He struggled with being. Circumstances changed, and he found a new happiness in another state. After carefully weighing the options of staying and going, he chose to go. Packing his moving truck was painful, saying goodbye with his promise of frequent visits was painful. Our worn and tattered ankle bracelets that had weathered the best and the worst were a testament to a human attachment that desperately held its threads together. This adventure was one that wouldn't last. His health declined, and his partner living across the street from me couldn't keep taking him back.

If you have ever known a person who dances on the edges of a fast and furious life that their body just can't keep up with, you will understand the hellish cycle of ache and agony that those who loved my friend went through, including me. The phone calls got further and further apart, the excuses got more and more grandiose and the patience of not being told the truth ran thin. I cried for him more times than I care to admit. More times than I thought was possible I believed the stories that my friend was doing well. He was depressed and spinning out of control, doing things that were harmful to him and those around him. Many times I planned to scoop him up out of his "Happy," "Fun," "Worth it all," "Pitiful," "Sick" life and bring him to my home to force him back to health, to reality. I never acted on that, not that he would come anyway, but I did eventually learn that his "sickness" could not be cured. My friend proclaimed that he had cancer and that his only option at this point was to go home to live with his mother, three states away. He said he was going there to die.

I am left with the guilt that the years of his stories and embellishments and need for telling a grand tale left me lacking much sympathy. I had heard the woes of a desperate man who craved notice for his depravity and disguised it as illness so many times that I had already turned my head when the stories turned real and deadly.

I will not retell all of the details of his painful decline. I will only recount that he often called me with joyful accounts of some amazing job opportunity that days later ended in some scheme that the company or the employees that worked there had executed to cause his separation with the establishment. My friend was talented on so many levels and to watch, in action, the deterioration of his gifts as he blamed the masses for his failure, was heartbreaking. I cannot fault him, he grappled with so much. He was a young and handsome man who loved other men in a world that hated men who loved other men.

I remember the shame I felt whenever my friend would call and tell me of his worsening ailments because I could not always believe the tale. I hated that in the background of my thoughts was an eye-roll and "whatever" types of feeling. It was always dramatic, he was always weakening, yet he always had more days to detail the fallout he was overcoming. I stopped answering his calls every time his name popped up on my phone and only chose to talk to him when I knew I had the strength to be present and encouraging.

Then, his partner decided to go pay him a visit at his mother's house. He wanted to see in person, like the rest of us, how dire my bestie's situation had become and he promised he would come back with a report of how worried we should be. When he returned he was in a state of grimness that could only mean that there had to be some truth behind my friend's account of his imminent death. I was shown pictures of the deterioration of a once proud and lively man. He bore no hair on his head, his clothes hung off his bones like a wet sack. I was caught between waiting for the next tale and hating myself for not rushing to his sickbed.

One sunny afternoon, I sat on my back porch enjoying the warmth of the sun when his name popped up on my phone, I didn't answer. Moments later I listened to the message that he left for me. He sounded so happy and spoke clearly and stated that he had some great news! He ended with an "I love you" and "I cherish our friendship". After listening to his message, I called him back right away hoping to talk to the jovial friend that I missed so dearly. Indeed, he was his old self, cheery and fun-loving. He amused me with his quick-witted jokes and vibrant conversation. He had just left the hospital for a refill of his meds. We had talked about his funeral many times before, but he went over the details with me once again. He wanted the black onyx casket, he was to be dressed in his finest suit and designer glasses, in his hand he would clutch his precious cell phone and I was to embalm his body.

Then he told me his exciting news. He had just been hired to work for a local flower shop. He would be arranging bouquets of flowers for birthdays, weddings, and funerals, which was among his many talents. I was given a detailed account of his interview and how fabulous the owner of the shop was and that his first day was tomorrow, the next day. He was so dedicated to this opportunity and certain that he could keep this position and finally thrive in this small country town where he now lived. When the conversation was over I hung up the phone thinking he was finally on the upswing again and flourishing enough and that I didn't need to worry for him for the moment. I was so wrong.

Speaking of the dead by Chelsea L. Tolman

It was the very next day that I received a call from his partner that my bestie had been found dead. He had died in his sleep, discovered resting peacefully in his bed, no longer breathing. The news was devasting and unexpected. I had just talked to him! He was happy and sounded so healthy. So many times I had expected the news of his death, only because he always tiptoed on the edge of life with partying and depression. But when I received that phone call it took the air from my lungs. The zipping memories of laughs and smiles and fear and anger that had I shared with him and our friends flashed over and over in my head. You always think that the best years of a friendship, or any relationship for that matter will never end. The late-night talks on the back porch, watching the fashion shows as he paraded in front of us all to show off new shirts and jackets and shoes. The bonfires with all of us giggling together and the flames dancing as a happy background to our moments. No more phone calls of fabulous jobs that he would be fabulous at and promised to keep this time. No more stories of whatever ailments were harming him at the moment. No more heartbreaking calls begging for visitors or confessing that he had made a terrible mistake and he just wanted to come back home.

I spoke with his mother about embalming him. She relayed to me that the funeral home had already performed the procedure after they picked him up from the medical examiner's office and it was too late for me to fly out and help.

I was managing a funeral home in another state when he died. The job was one that was almost impossible to take any time off from. So I made a plan to drive the ten hours there, attend the funeral, get a couple of hours of sleep and then drive the ten hours again to return back to work.

I woke up hours before sunrise on the day of his funeral and drove to this small town, where my friend would be buried. It was like I was in a dream. As I drove the miles and the sun started to rise I wondered if I had imagined it all. I was delirious with emotion and lack of sleep and grappling with the reality of what I was doing. I was wicked tired but so full of adrenaline that my body felt out of place with itself.

As I approached the address for the funeral home I was overwhelmed with what was waiting for me in that building. I was not ready. I could not stop the car. I drove right past and burst into tears while looking watching the funeral home as I drove past, where my friend lay waiting for my arrival decked out in his finest no doubt, and dead. My friend was dead. I could see his lifeless body in my head, I could feel his cold skin. I couldn't imagine walking into that building with people all around me and having the energy to stifle my grief. My anger. My guilt. I wanted those people to leave so that I could be with him alone and explain why I never came to see him in the darkest moments of his life that were real and not fabricated. These people were in the way and rude for being so present when I needed them to just go away.

Then, I was a funeral director, I had seen this before. So many funerals I had directed where I heard from the guests in attendance about the one person who never came to see the deceased while they were living, yet that very same person was the one who was making the most fuss and carrying on about their own grief. I felt that I had turned into that person. I drove to a convenience store on a corner up the road and one block over from the funeral home, I did not want to be on the same road as my dead friend at that moment. I didn't want to be in the same town.

I needed gas, I needed some water, I needed sleep and I needed my friend to be alive so that I could go visit him just like he had begged me to for so many months. Eventually I couldn't stall any longer. I pulled myself back into my car. First one leg, sit on the seat, then the other leg, adjust the mirror. The seat belt needed latching, so I did that. I was thirsty, so I gulped from my water bottle. Next was to close the car door but first I needed to make sure I was really ready.

119

Speaking of the dead by Chelsea L. Tolman

I should use the restroom again. Splash more water on my face. I was so tired. Every movement was a chore, my limbs felt caked in wet mud, heavy and sluggish as I undid the seat belt and ambled back to the restroom, ignoring what I was certain were sidelong glances at my state of suffering. I made a final check of the things that I felt were necessary to stall just another moment.

Finally, I had myself in my car, buckled, door closed and turned the car key to rumble the engine to life. I drove to the funeral home. I parked my car where the lot attendants told me to, a job I had performed for so many other grieving people. Now, I was the one grieving and their instructions were confusing and impatient. A teaching moment for the future. In that moment I went from a total mess, grieving my friend, to funeral home manager. I felt like I should instruct these young kids on how to perform their job of directing traffic well enough to pack a hundred cars in a fashion that would allow for a smooth transition to the cemetery when the funeral was over. I cased the parking lot, the exit from the chapel, the direction of where the procession needed to go. I needed to let it go. Funeral directors are terrible funeral guests, even if we are professional enough to keep our thoughts to ourselves, we still observe the way a funeral is run by others. I felt I should be in charge but I was not and so I kept my thoughts to myself, exited my vehicle and walked the walk to front door.

The funeral home was buzzing with people. They were moving about unorganized and loud. I didn't recognize anyone there. I kept walking until I saw his name and felt more shock and grief, this was his name, on a placard, in a funeral home, hovering just above an open book for the guests to sign. I made my way to there. The light that glared down on the book was hot as I tried to scribble my name and leave a sweet message for his mother. I then walked into the room jammed with people smiling and talking. And then I saw across the room bits of the silver and black casket, through the throng of bodies I also caught a glimpse of dark spiky hair peeking over the lip of the box. I excused myself through the jumble of people seemingly intent on preventing me from seeing my dead friend and just before I approached my destination I was stopped by a hand on my arm. I turned to see who could be so rude in preventing me from finishing my quest. It was his mother. She grabbed me in a full-bodied hug sobbing, "You came, you came!" I could only squeeze her tighter as I held my own emotions in my throat. She let go of me and then wrapped one arm around my waist as we walked to the casket containing the body of her sweet, baby boy.

Speaking of the dead by Chelsea L. Tolman

Clumps of ash choked my throat as I tried to breathe, to swallow, to not break into shards of grief. My vision was blurred as it was confirmed that my friend was still and cold. So many times, I have stood at a casket after fussing and tucking and straightening, looking at the person lying inside with my friend standing next to me. He would tell me how good a job I did preparing this person, "You have a gift," "You are an artist," "The family is going to be so pleased" He would say "One day you will prepare my body and you better make me look just as good!"

Now I stand at his casket that I didn't help pick out, looking at his body that I didn't embalm and assessing the folds in his suit that I did not dress him in. And he looked good. At that moment it did not matter that I did not do these things for him, at that moment I was not a funeral director, I was grief-stricken and mourning for my dear friend.

I left his mother and scanned the room to see if I could find my friends partner. I found him across the room talking to a gentleman and so I made my approach. Once he saw me he grabbed me in a huge bear hug and couldn't believe that I had driven the ten hours in only ten hours. And then the introductions started. It was a furious affair of being dragged from person to person, all of these people I did not know, yet when introduced with my name almost every time these

122

people responded "Chelsea! You are Chelsea, his best friend? I have heard so much about you," "He loved you so much," "He always talked about you." This was flattering. This was uncomfortable. I was this person who everyone knew as his best friend. He talked about me, shared our stories, made me up to be like this amazing angel that he looked up to and I had left him to die all alone.

After the funeral, we all drove in procession to the cemetery, a trek I had made so many times to so many cemeteries, never before driving in a car trailing behind the hearse. The cars snaked through stop lights and around the turns and bends of the small-town blocks to end at the snow-laden cemetery with only one dark patch of earth dotting our destination, my friend's grave. I didn't feel the cold although I am certain it was biting. I don't remember much of the graveside service either other than I was placed up in front of the crowd, standing with the family, right where I was told I belonged.

I can still see him in his casket, I imagine him lying enclosed in his box, sealed in a concrete case, buried in the earth. He is dressed to the nines, pressed, clean shaven with perfectly spiked hair and clutching his beloved cell phone. On occasion, for months, I would send him a text letting him know of my sorrow. My guilt. I could imagine him lying there

123

still and lifeless clutching his phone to his chest as it lit up his darkness with my messages, never read. Eventually the batteries would go dead, and my confessions and heartbreak would only be sent into the digital wasteland of regret, and grief.

Speaking of the dead by Chelsea L. Tolman

LEFT BEHIND

It was a beautiful spring day in the South. Blue skies and warm sunshine graced the many people arriving at the mortuary for the funeral that was about to start. Guests were wearing their spring finery, the ladies in shorter dresses and open toed shoes, the men casting their jackets aside, favoring the more casual dress shirt and tie look. I knew ahead of time that it was to be a large funeral but still had no idea what was in store for me that day. The deceased was an older gentleman who was well known in the community and the widow as sweet as candy, elderly and slow yet she was full of smiles, gentleness. As people were entering the large chapel they would place their bags or children on the pews, saving their spot for the service, then wander off to mingle with the rest of the crowd. I noticed that the seats were filling up fast, so I quickly rounded up my staff and gave them instructions to bring out our folding chairs to accommodate the ever-growing flood of people. I then ran to the back of the mortuary and turned the air conditioner on full blast to hopefully stave off the heat that so many people in one room would generate. Eventually we had to start telling new arrivals that there just wasn't any more seating in the chapel, even with folding chairs crammed into every available space. Thankfully there

125

was a room adjacent to the chapel that had a TV screen and sound system set up to display the service as it was happening.

The crowd was dense and unaccommodating. Moving through the throng carrying our folding chairs should be a new Olympic event. The people talked loudly with each other in groups and ignored our requests of passage to set down the next row of seating, giving me and my staff a sidelong glance before rolling their eyes and continuing with their ever-important conversations, like there was not a funeral about to take place, like we were not doing this just for them! As we set up the adjacent room with folding chairs, it seemed the moment a chair was set down it was immediately filled with a bag, jacket or child, even before the chair was properly in place. It was a frantic, frustrating affair. Finally, the flow of people coming in to the mortuary slowed and it seemed that we had enough seats for everyone in attendance.

With my face flush and glistening from sweat and my veins still full of adrenaline, I walked up to the pulpit to address the mass of people and announce that the funeral was about to begin. I am small in stature, yet powerful in personality and in the event that I need to get the attention of a

Speaking of the dead by Chelsea L. Tolman

crowd I am usually able to speak forcefully enough to get everyone's attention. Today, this was not the case. The chatter in the room was so loud that even with the help of the microphone and sound system, I could barely hear my own voice. And of course, being short and small, no one even noticed that I was standing up there on the stage. As I scanned the chapel from my platform, the sea of people talking and milling about was like watching a bee hive that had been poked with a stick and I knew I had to be creative in getting the attention of the swarm. I again rallied my staff and soon had them all hopping from group to group announcing that the funeral was starting. Finally, as the word got around, the crowd started to quiet down and people took their seats and this time when I spoke into the mic, my voice could be heard and I was able to begin the funeral. Once my opening speech was finished, I handed the pulpit over to the clergy and happily took my leave of that room.

My staff and I made our way out to sit in a back room of the mortuary, fanning our heat from the previous mad dash of unfolding chairs and efforts at crowd control. We discussed in awe of the craziness we had just witnessed. Not that we hadn't been prepared for a large crowd, but that we were wholly unprepared for such a disorderly group of people.

We then discussed a strategy for moving all of these people to their cars so that we could get on the road to the cemetery in a timely fashion. Our plan was to have two staff members leave with the casket and pall bearers, then I was to exit behind them with the widow and immediate family members whisking them away to their vehicles before any of the guests could stop and talk to them, which always happened and always slowed progress. Once I was out of the chapel with the family, my staff would then announce to the congregation that the procession would be leaving soon and assist in ushering them quickly to their vehicles. The cars had been previously parked to efficiently exit the parking lot in one big line and the police escort was at the driveway waiting for my signal to leave. There were so many attendees that the cars wrapped around the building, making it impossible for me to see when everyone was settled in their cars, so, we had a plan. Once the cars were all occupied, my staff would give me signal and I could then give the police escort the go ahead to exit.

Almost everything went as planned. I successfully escorted the family to their vehicles and watched from the parking lot as the mob of people filed out of the chapel and in turn got into their own cars. I was watching for the signal when I saw one of my staff standing at the side of the building and raise his arm in my direction. I took that as a sign that we were ready. I gave the police the go ahead, got myself into the hearse and we started the exit of the parking lot. As I looked in the mirrors to see behind me, as I always do to get a sense of the procession following, I noticed there was a flurry of people rushing around like straggling wild bees and my coworkers trying to flag me down and several of the cars behind me were not moving! But it was too late, the police cars were out in the street, the procession had begun. I slowed my pace as much as I could to give time for people to get in line, but we were on our way and there was no stopping it. Now, it could be that I was just anxious to get moving, or it could be that he was just scratching his head, either way, it was apparent that my staff did not actually give me a signal and all of the people were not in their cars ready to go.

Once we reached the cemetery, we had to wait longer than usual for everyone to arrive. It was hot and humid and there was not enough room under the tent to shade the crowd from the blaring sun. It was miserable for everyone. The elderly wife was so gracious and patient, opting to wait for everyone to arrive before starting the graveside, gently fanning herself with our provided funeral home fan. We did eventually have the graveside and when it was over the wife and family seemed very happy with how everything had been handled, which is really the ultimate goal.

Once I got back to the mortuary my staff and I had a meeting about what had happened, what we learned from the experience and how to handle similar situations in the future. I also learned that the deceased man's own sister had been left behind, she was not in the procession! She had gone back inside to use the restroom and upon her return the parking lot was empty. She then made the choice not to go to the cemetery, fearing that she would get lost and miss the graveside anyway. All in all, even with the frantic rushing of unfolding chairs, shuffling people and a missing sister, this really wasn't the worst that could happen in a funeral service, at least the casket arrived where it was supposed to. And a bit of advice, when directing a funeral service, assure you have clear, recognizable signals with your staff, because you never know who might get left behind.

TWO MAN COT

I was given the task of picking up a man at the medical examiner's office and transport him to one of our other locations. We were really busy that day, every employee was rushing about handling some type of funeral home task. I was instructed to use one of our vans since the transport hearse was being used by another employee. I was to drive the van from the front of the mortuary to the side garage entrance where a coworker was getting a cot ready for me.

As I backed the van up the driveway I saw my coworker. He was rolling out a cot from the back of the garage. I had seen these cots back there before, lined up nicely, covered in plastic, waiting for someone to need them. I assumed they were extras just waiting for a day like to today when they would be brought in to the sunshine to be used for the purpose they were made. I thought nothing more about it. My coworker gestured for me to stay in the van, he opened the back door, shoved the cot in then motioned for me to get on the road.

Once I arrived at the medical examiner's office, I backed into a narrow driveway that ended at a concrete ramp.

Speaking of the dead by Chelsea L. Tolman

At the top of the ramp was a dead-bolted metal door and a door bell mounted on the building to the right of the door. Procedure was to ring the bell and wait for someone to open the door. This could take anywhere from two to twenty minutes depending on how busy they were that day. I got out of the van, rang the bell and then waited. Thankfully I didn't have to wait long. Soon an employee, whom I was familiar with (he was one of the friendly ones,) came out and walked with me to the back of the van and just to be helpful he removed the cot for me and together we walked inside. After he graciously assisted me in transferring the man onto my cot (he was one of the very few who would do this), he walked me outside, loaded the cot into my van and I hit the road.

When I arrived at the funeral home, I backed up the van as close to the embalming room door as I could (it was located at the rear of the funeral home). The building was red brick with white trim. Extending from the brick wall was a concrete slab that reached about five feet and ended in a black asphalt parking lot that stepped down two inches lower than the concrete. There were large white columns located every ten feet or so to support an awning that protected the back entrance doors from the elements. I parked my van in between two of the columns that were located on either side of the embalming room door.

After getting out of the van, I unlocked the door to the embalming room and propped it open so that I could easily roll the cot inside. I then went to the back of the van and proceeded to pull out the cot, just like I normally would. The way I was used to a cot working is, you hold a lever at one end to release one set of wheels, pull it out halfway then let go of the lever to lock the wheels in the down position. Then continue pulling the cot and the second set of wheels would automatically unfold and lock into place. Now being supported by both sets of wheels the cot could be safely rolled away from the back of the vehicle. So, I did just that, held the lever, pulled the cot out halfway and the wheels locked. I released the lever and confidently continued to pull the cot, trusting the second set of wheels would unfold and lock as they had with other cots a dozen times previously. However, before I realized what was happening, as I pulled, the other end of the cot suddenly slipped off the end of the bumper and slammed onto the asphalt with an awful, clattering crash! The second set of wheels firmly folded in place.

I stood there shocked. Quite unsure of what had just happened. I looked around and contemplated my situation. There were two things that I had to consider immediately. One, was that the end of the cot sitting on the ground was where the head of the man was located, meaning his feet were up in the air on the end of the cot that operated correctly. Having a body laying in this position will cause the blood, no longer circulating, to gravitate towards his head. Allowing this to happen for very long would mean the man's face could swell and become discolored, making a difficult situation for the embalmer. The second consideration was that it was the height of summer, during the hottest part of the day, in the South. This hot, muggy weather can cause the decomposition process to accelerate at an alarming rate. I had to get this man flat and inside and fast!

So, I did what anyone would do, I went to the side of the cot on the ground and tried to lift it straight up, hoping the wheels would unfold, allowing me to resume getting this man inside. But the wheels remained firmly locked in place. I tried again, straining with my back and legs desperate to get the wheels to release, yet still the wheels refused to budge. So, my next thought was that maybe I could lift the cot just high enough to get the cot back into the van, where I could turn on the AC and then get some help. I lifted the grounded end of the cot again, straining to get it onto the bumper of the van but to no avail. I was just not tall enough to lift such a heavy weight that high.

I was wearing a polo shirt made of thick knitted cotton. I wore long khaki pants and a baseball cap and it was hot as hell! I took out my cell phone and called the funeral home. Even though I was at the back door, I wanted to avoid walking into the building and risk a family seeing me dressed casually, disheveled and drenched in sweat. Unfortunately, I was greeted by the answering service. No one was there. No one could help me. I had to quickly figure out a solution on my own. I decided I would put the entire cot on the ground and drag the whole damn thing into the embalming room. There were metal poles on each corner of the cot that reached below the folded wheels, making it impossible to simply wheel the grounded cot inside. Just imagine, young girl, mid-twenties, red faced and sweaty, dragging a cot on the concrete, one inch at a time. If you ever want this experience take a sheet of plywood, attached a metal leg to each corner, pile two hundred pounds of weight on it, then drag it on a concrete surface.

Speaking of the dead by Chelsea L. Tolman

My first challenge was the difference in height between the asphalt and concrete slab. To get the cot up over the lip, I gave it a good heft and push, which made a bone-tingling screech and gouged the concrete. But, I couldn't worry about that, this body needed to get out of the heat and into a temperature-controlled room, and quickly. So, for the sake of protecting the body, I continued pulling. Every inch of progress resulted in a line gouged in the concrete and made a terrible shriek with every pull. Shriek. Rest my arms. Shriek. Rest my legs, one excruciating inch at a time.

I neared the threshold of the door and wrenched the first set of locked wheels over the threshold and onto the tile floor of the embalming room. This turned the previous shriek into a high-pitched squeal as the metal strained against the tile. Squeal. Rest. Squeal and then I stopped... I had a tingling feeling, like I was being watched. I looked up from my hunched position and from under my baseball cap and through trickles of sweat, I saw them. My coworkers. Two in a hearse and two in a van, they were just coming back from a funeral service. They had stopped their cars to watch the new girl dragging the cot into the embalming room... laughing hysterically of course. I stood up, relieved to have people there to help, then I imagined what this must look like and couldn't help but join them in wild laughter. And I laughed because of the sheer embarrassment of my situation.

The doors of the cars began to open but these men were laughing so hard that getting out of the vehicles was a feat in itself. It was like watching drunk men trying to get their footing after riding a roller coaster. They were falling all over each other. Once they settled down and after some discussion, through their tears of laughter, the men explained to me that the cot I was using was an old two-man cot. This meant that there was a lever on each end, meant for two people to operate at the same time. Or if you were by yourself, the end of the cot you pull out first had two levers, one to release then lock one set of wheels and one to release and then lock the other set of wheels.

My lesson for that day was always know your equipment before using it. With the help of my coworkers, we got the cot raised up on all four wheels and the cot carrying the man was rolled normally into the embalming room. It took no time at all before the entire company had learned of what happened. The jokes followed of course and lasted for months.

Speaking of the dead by Chelsea L. Tolman

<u>WRONG CHURCH, WRONG CHURCH, WRONG CHURCH</u>

No matter how hard we try, funeral directors make mistakes. And it seems inevitable that once one thing has gone wrong with a funeral or its planning, then it just snowballs during the entire process and everything else goes wrong too. Then the more careful and intentional you are to make things go smoothly, the worse it gets! Like suddenly your hands are covered in ink and everything you touch gets a smudge. Sometimes it's small things and the family never knows and sometimes it's a big thing and not only does the family know but all of their friends know as well.

I met with the family of a younger man (mid-fifties'). This family was great! We hit it off from the beginning. We had some laughing moments and some tender moments, and everything was going smoothly for the circumstances. During the arrangements I went over the details of the service, day, time, place etc. I wrote everything down finalized it all with the family and then sent them home. I sat down to my desk and completed all of my tasks, called the cemetery, ordered staff and cars for the service, ordered the casket and vault and called the family's clergyman to coordinate when to have the church open for us.

I was scheduled to be off work for the next couple of days, so I carefully went over everything ahead of time to make sure that nothing was left undone. Filled in death certificate information, put the day and time of the family dressing in the scheduling book, I made sure that everything was in order so that my coworkers knew what was to happen while I was away. I then wrote out the obituary according to the instructions the family gave me, and I sent it to the family for final approval before I sent it to the newspapers. At the end of the day, paperwork filled out, cemetery confirmed, clergy and church building confirmed, obituary approved, paid and sent to the paper. I then went home, confidant that nothing was out of place or left undone.

On the day of the funeral my staff and I showed up the mortuary early and loaded the cars with everything we would need for the day, register book, programs, flowers, tissues, lamps, TV and DVD player etc., then placed the casket carrying the deceased man into the hearse, checked the address of the church and made our way out. It was winter time and lightly snowing, the roads were covered in slush thick and muddy that clung to our tires and made the drive slippery and slimy and slow. We found our church and pulled into the parking lot. There was one car already there parked way in the back corner of the lot (usually that meant someone had opened the building for us to unload our supplies for the service). We noticed that the sidewalks were shoveled and ready for the funeral. We walked around the building, found the open door and let ourselves in. We busied ourselves with unpacking all of our equipment, including the casket. We set up the flowers got the DVD playing on the TV screen, set out the register book, programs and tissues for the guests and then sat and waited for the family to get there.

It was unusually quiet at this church. Normally by this time more church members were there, setting up tables for the luncheon and making sure the trash was emptied but we were the only ones there. It was getting closer to the time for the visitation to start and still not even the family was there. Of course, we thought nothing of it, we were at the right address, the building was open and the sidewalks were shoveled, other than the lack of people, everything was as normal.

Speaking of the dead by Chelsea L. Tolman

I received a phone call from a coworker and said the family had called and asked where we were?! Um, at the church, all set up and waiting for them, where were they?! I got the number for the family and called quickly, curious as to what had happened. After some discussion, it was determined that over the course of the couple of days I was gone, the family had changed the location of the funeral and no one had told me or changed it in the book! I was mortified. There are few things that cause panic quicker than for a funeral director to realize we are at the wrong church and now will be late getting set up for the funeral! My staff and I quickly started loading everything back up and got in our cars as fast as possible. I had written down this new location and got the GPS running as we exited the parking lot, thank goodness it was close to where we already were. We turned into the new parking lot and there was no one there! The parking lot and sidewalks piled high with fresh snow! Something was wrong. I called the family back only to be told that there were 4 churches all in the same area and GPS couldn't find 2 of them, one of which I needed to be at an hour ago! The deceased man's son got on the phone and directed me turn by turn to the correct location. As we finally got to the right church, the entire family and several of their friends were crowded on the sidewalk to watch our cars pull in, an hour late! It was mortifying.

Everyone there got busy helping us unload the cars for the second time and soon we had everything set up, again, for the funeral. I apologized to the family stating I was not aware of the location change. They, now that panic was over, laughed it off and said that the man was late for everything else so why not his funeral. The rest of the day went on without a hitch, everyone was happy, and the man was successfully buried as scheduled

So, lesson learned, communication is everything!

WARD OF THE STATE

One day I got a call from a nurse to come pick up a gentleman at the hospital. I thought nothing of it as this was the routine. I asked the nurse the pertinent questions, name, room number, family contact. This is when she hesitated for a moment, then informed me that there was no family left and that the man's affairs were being handled by the state. She also told me that she called my mortuary due to a note in his file that his funeral was pre-planned with us. I was given the number of the person in charge of his matters and informed her that I would call her back once I had more details. After I hung up I looked for the file with the name I was given and found that he did in fact plan a funeral with us, and a grand one! High-end casket, top of line vault and a flower allowance that could make a bride envious, and then he was to be buried at a local country church cemetery. Everything seemed to be in order aside from the fact that none of it had been paid for, it was only the man's wishes on paper, nothing more. Normally when there isn't any family to pay for services, the state handles the funeral arrangements and typically chooses the funeral home they would be released to. Armed with this information I called the woman handling his affairs and again started asking questions, were there no children? siblings? cousins? anybody? Then she told me the sad tale of this man.

He had never married and never had any children, but he did have two siblings who had taken care of him for a while. The brother sadly passed away which left only his sister to care for him, she herself getting older and less able to handle his care. Eventually the man ended up in a facility that could see to his needs full time as his health declined. His sister came now and again to visit with him and brought him fresh clothing, food and such. She would take him on outings for lunch or to the Zoo and even to the funeral home to make his final arrangements. Then, she stopped coming. After some time, the facility wondered what happened to her and tried to get in contact with her, the phone number they had was disconnected and it seemed that she had just, disappeared. This is when the state got involved and he was assigned a social worker to handle his care and affairs.

He lived for several more years, during that time he developed dementia and was forgetting more and more of his life. I was told he used to talk about his siblings fondly and always asked about his missing sister. The social worker, who was originally assigned to care for him, moved on or got a promotion or something and so it was reassigned to the woman I was speaking with. She said that when she took over his case (about a year prior), he remembered very little and was no help in finding any relatives that may still be living. She did another search for the missing sister and found that she had passed away some years ago. She also had never married or had any children and had lived alone. She had left pre-planned funeral arrangements of her own, an immediate burial (where the funeral home is to bury without any family or friends present). She was now buried in the same church cemetery as her brother was to be interred upon his death. Thus, her mysterious disappearance was solved.

The social worker and I talked about the grand funeral plans he had made, and I informed her how it was only his wishes and wasn't funded. Then she had news that blew me away. The man had set aside the money to pay for his funeral and then some! The state was in charge of his finances and would be paying for whatever he wanted in his funeral plan, with plenty of money left over. I told her that it didn't seem right to have such an extravagant amount of money paid out for a funeral that might not even have any guests since I was certain he ordered these services for his friends and family, but was told that her instructions were to provide all of the services he ordered. After we exchanged some more contact information, I hung up the phone with the social worker and called the nurse back to let her know that I would in fact be handling this man's funeral and that I would come to pick him up shortly.

I remember making the arrangements. All the paperwork was signed through email and fax with the social worker (we never met in person). I called the church and asked if they could provide a clergy to say a few words. No one remembered who he was as it had been so long since he had come to church, but they agreed to provide us with an officiant. I ordered the metal casket painted light blue, and the vault I had painted silver to match the hardware of the casket, just as he had requested. The allowance given for the flowers was more than enough for a spectacular display of color and texture. I sent a check to the cemetery for opening and closing (fees to dig the grave and then fill it in after the funeral). I even printed an obituary with the little information I had. After all was said and done, it was to be a lovely funeral! I had him embalmed and dressed him in the dark brown suit he picked from the mortuary clothing line (most mortuaries have burial clothing for purchase) and I gave him clean brown socks and a pressed white shirt. Once I had him in the casket I fussed over straightening his tie and pulling any folds out of the shirt and jacket. The brown suit was a nice contrast to the stark white interior of the pale blue casket with bright silver hardware.

Then it was time for the funeral. I remember getting there early to set everything up and deep down I hoped that someone who knew him would see his obituary and be there to fill a chair. It was a warm spring day, the grass was green, and the small white country church stood on a hill overlooking the cemetery. Blue skies with wispy white clouds and the occasional lazy bird floating above was the background to our green funeral tent. The light blue casket stood on top of the silver vault which accented the handles brilliantly. The flower arrangement of bright oranges and deep reds gave the lazy Spring setting a burst of excitement.

The clergy walked down from the church and we spoke of things he would say and then a car pulled up and a woman got out. Hoping beyond hope that this person would be a friend of the deceased and would have something new to add to our meager eulogy. I introduced myself as she walked up only to discover that this woman was none other than the social worker with whom I had been working with! I was touched and surprised, she had taken her lunch break to attend the funeral of a man who she had only known through his fragmented recollections. We hugged and decided to wait a few moments more just in case someone else, anyone else showed up. "I was anticipating that nobody would come since his life ended in such a lonely state. I always find empty funerals to be sad, but I was prepared for this one."

About a month later I received another call from the social worker, she said that the extra money he had set aside for his funeral needed to be spent, their office was going to be audited and they couldn't have the money sitting 'idle in their account. So, we talked about some different options. Charity, donating it to the state or opening a fund for those who needed money for a funeral. All of these options, it seemed, did not fall under the guidelines of how the money could be spent. It had to go for his funeral expenses. Since he was buried at the church, I contacted the clergy there and asked if the church or cemetery could use a bench or tree or anything. He said the road was in serious disrepair and that they had been talking about putting a bench near the playground on the other side of the cemetery for weary parents to watch their children exhaust themselves. We also noticed that two of his family members' headstones were crumbling and in need of replacement. After some talking and planning it was determined that all of this fell within the strange guidelines.

All in all, the man paid for two new headstones, two granite benches with his name inscribed on each and what was left went towards a new road through the cemetery. This was indeed a tribute to and from the dead man, and one of the most expensive funerals I had ever directed!

SHE WAS MY BEST FRIEND

I recently read a book written by David Sedaris called "Let's Explore Diabetes With Owls." In one chapter he is talking about parenting and the difference between how parents raise children now compared to when he was young. In earlier times when you did something wrong you were punished for it and learned not to do it again or the next consequence was more severe and so on. More and more we see that parents are more becoming lenient, not wanting to be like their parents. It is almost a crime to spank or yell or say no to your kids. The children run the household and parents are afraid to anger them or they suffer the consequences and so on. I am one of the lucky kids raised with rules and structure. I fought it, I hated it, I railed and kicked and screamed about it but I learned. I respect others and their property, I earned my dollars with my own hands and do not expect others to pay or pave my way through life. I appreciate those lessons, I became an adult through these lessons. I understand a parent treating their child like they would have wanted when they grew up but it feels like there should be a balance between lenience and structure, parent and child.

Speaking of the dead by Chelsea L. Tolman

It's not easy to prepare a child for a funeral. They are small and smooth and fragile and they are dead. The young are naturally beautiful in a different way than the elderly. No laugh lines or sun spots. Age has not claimed the lip lines or strained the joints to turn and twist. It's like a sin almost to see them lying on my table for the preparation of their funeral. However, it is gratifying to place them gently in a casket, like a jewelry box for the perfect diamond or pearl. There is rarely a need for extra color to contour cheekbones or accentuate lashes, those things haven't experienced enough life to look aged.

There was a girl, thirteen years old, I met with the family before I ever knew what happened to her. As I started asking the family questions to learn who she was and how to serve them, I noticed that the mother was sad but in a different way. Her daughter had committed suicide and I have seen what that can do to a parent. Her grief was muted though, like someone hit the pause button on a VCR and it didn't take quite right so there is a slight jump in the stillness of the picture. She was obviously devastated, the tears flowed and the eyes sunk, yet there was something else. I asked to see a picture of her daughter and as she pulled out her phone and handed it to me she said, "She was my best friend." There it

Speaking of the dead by Chelsea L. Tolman

was, I still didn't get it yet but that phrase stayed with me. The girl was beautiful and the whole family made comments on how she looked so much older than she was. Every picture I was shown she was dressed to the nines, full makeup which was heavy on the eyes, short skirts, high heels and one picture with a drink in her hand. If I had not known better, I would have guessed her eighteen or twenty years old. In the mixture, there were pictures of her without the layers, stripped down to a thirteen-year-old child who needing nothing more than structure and rules to guide her in making good life decisions.

As we talked about her funeral the family insisted on having a friend come and do her makeup. She was beautiful, angelic in her youngness. I looked at her for a long time. Asked her why she was dead-even though I had a suspicion. Shortly before the friend was to come and do the make up the girl's mother called and said that her friend was too distraught and could not do it and asked if I would just do it instead. She sent me a picture and strict instructions on how perfect and bold her daughters make up must be. How was I to do this? This thirteen-year-old child lying in front of me, bathed and dressed, so beautiful and perfect just the way she was. And I am asked to mar her sweet face with thick globs of red and black. I remembered the pictures of her daughter with skirts

153

and heels designed for sexual appeal, the thick black lines around her stunning eyes and lips lined and red to appear bigger, poutier, kissable. I struggled through every step. This should not have happened, and I should not have to be doing this.

During the funeral the mother got up and spoke. She talked again about her best friend and how the neighbor kids loved to hang out at her house. It was hard to listen to her mother tell me how they got her on birth control. It was hard to see the pictures of her drinking while posing in a slinky dress. It was hard to hear her mother stand at the podium in front of all of these people and tell them that she let her daughter run her own life. She couldn't tell her no. She said she couldn't stop her from drinking and having sex, so instead she encouraged it and gave her tips and helped her because she was a good mother.

Thirteen-year-old's haven't gained the coping skills for complicated adult situations like sex. Their bodies are still growing and drugs and alcohol only damage the growth they have left to accomplish. These situations are difficult enough when you reach an appropriate age to experience them. I am angry at the mother for putting me in a position to have to foul such a beautiful child. I am angry at her that she didn't have the courage to be a mother and chose instead to be a best friend. I am not a mother and I cannot help but think that if this girl had been pushed to behave like a thirteen-year-old, she would still be here and still be her mother's best friend but in a different way.

THE WEDDING GOWN

Every mortuary has different procedures for shipping and receiving deceased bodies. I was relatively new to this particular mortuary and was working with, what we call in the industry, a "ship in" (where a person dies in one state and then needs to be transported to another state for funeral services and/or burial). Because I was still new to the procedures of this mortuary, which had multiple locations, I just operated in the manner I was used to and had the woman brought directly to the location where her services were to take place. The way it was supposed to work though was that all of the bodies were to be sent to a central location. There they would be checked and prepared and then transported to whichever location their services were going to be at. I am licensed director/embalmer and skilled enough to prepare any deceased in any manner and was confident that I could ensure this woman was ready for public viewing. At least that was what I thought.

Once the service had brought her to me I took her in a back room where there was space to work in. I untied the straps that held the container, containing the casket. My first shock was that this casket was almost certainly custom painted, giving levity to the detail her family was expecting. It was a bright, cherry red and glossy like a brand-new mustang. I reveled at how striking it was compared to the pastel metals and simple woods that I was used to. Then, I opened the casket.

To my horror, the woman had deteriorated badly, and fluid had leaked everywhere! I was told by her husband and son previously that she would be wearing her wedding gown from when she was married 30 years before! I was faced with a woman dressed in a white micro velvet wedding gown and cream, satin casket interior all stained in pink liquid.

I set out to look for supplies. I was unfamiliar with this mortuary and searched everywhere for what I needed to start cleaning the mess, only to realized that this location did not stock the provisions necessary to handle what I was faced with at this moment. To top it off, this all happened on a Sunday which meant that the mortuary was closed and the only staff available was our first call team (they pick up the deceased when a death occurs) and the person answering the phones (and they could not help at all). The family was scheduled to arrive in about three hours to see this woman who was their wife, mother and grandmother and then begin a viewing for her friends and family in the area.

I stared in disbelief at the drenched cloth of the casket and the treasured wedding gown, realizing I was sadly unequipped to fix this problem. I took a moment to gather myself because somehow, I had to find a solution. I had thankfully taken my day off to go to be at the mortuary and make sure everything was ready, otherwise this would have been discovered by a part-time staff member, making the situation an even bigger disaster.

I quickly called the first call team and, luckily, they happened to be at our central location and were just now getting back from transporting another decedent to that location. I gave them a list of the supplies that I needed and then, as I waited for them to arrive, I started the cleanup procedure. I took off the gown of micro velvet and used a chemical called dry wash (a solution used in dry cleaning) to clean the stains, I then scrubbed the interior of the casket with the supplies I had at hand. About forty minutes later my savior arrived, only to find out that he had mistakenly left the bag of requested supplies at the other location! It was a simple, unintentional mistake yet, the family of this woman was now scheduled to arrive in about an hour and a half! So, in a flurry of chemicals, scrubbing and a blow dryer I was able to sufficiently get the wedding gown washed and mostly dried and the casket interior cleaned. I then found the spot where the fluid had leaked out of and sealed it up with what I had. Once she was freshly dressed and arranged in the casket, I applied fresh makeup, added some curl to her hair and, only just in time, this woman was ready and I thought she looked beautiful.

The family arrived, and I greeted them in the lobby. They were all dressed silk suits, dresses and heels. Not a penny was spared in their attire. Coifed and primped as if going out for a night on the town. As I walked the family into the viewing room, I strained to see any hint of the disaster that had originally come to me in a shipping box and thankfully there was none and the family none the wiser.

In the end the family was thrilled, which meant that I was thrilled, tragedy averted, and the world turned once again. The next day we laid this woman to rest. Beautiful, pristine, in a glossy red casket dressed in her treasured white wedding gown. May she now rest in peace.

Speaking of the dead by Chelsea L. Tolman

A BALL OF TWIN

My career as a funeral director started out intensely. I had so many great experiences in a very short period of time. I consider myself lucky in this. This story happened when I was fairly new to the industry and really new to embalming on my own.

One night I was called to pick up an elderly woman from her home. As with most night calls, I drug myself out of bed, donned the trademark black funeral suit and arranged my hair as best I could with bleary, sleep deprived eyes. I met a coworker at the mortuary to retrieve the hearse and cot and of course talked about how we were to wake up, jokes or coffee? We pulled up to the house and I alone made my way to the front door while my coworker waited in the car for instructions. I was greeted with a smile and was invited to come in. As I entered the house, there were pictures of the family everywhere. It was a clean, well put together home with lots of love surrounding everything.

The children and grandchildren were gathered in the living room, quietly talking amongst themselves. They were all in different manners of dress, some pajamas, some

Speaking of the dead by Chelsea L. Tolman

disheveled street clothes (probably from being called out of bed at such a late hour). I sat down and started asking questions. I like to get to know something about the family and the deceased before leaving with such precious cargo. They told me that she had been a great mother, grandmother and wife. She kept the family together and was gentle and always kind. They were saddened about the loss yet recognized that she had lived to be 99 years old. They explained that she had lived a full yet simple country life, and that she had been ready to go for months. She was in pain and missed her husband.

They talked about how she had never been to a doctor, ever. Not even to deliver her babies (all of her children had been born at home). After my coworker and I placed her on the cot, we said goodbye to the family and made our way back to the funeral home to start the embalming procedure. To continue gaining experience in handling embalming on my own it was determined that I would go solo this time, with help just around the corner if I needed it. As I made the incision and started looking for vessels, I was deterred by a huge gray mass! It was spongy and thick and it was intertwined around everything. Muscle, tendon, blood vessels. And the more I sorted through the mass the bigger I saw it was. I was fascinated. So I started to remove it as intact as I could, cutting around the normal tissue and vessels until eventually I freed the glob. I placed it on the table next to the woman, the only sound in the room was the water splashing down the table from the hose. It was the size of a large peach pit, and I started dissecting it and pulling at it. After some time of looking and analyzing I came realize that it was hair! A mass of hair and bits of hardened... somethings. As I took this anomaly apart I couldn't help but think about what the family had told me, that this woman had never seen a doctor in all of her 99 years.

Not sure what to think about this, I brought in my coworker in to look at it with me "Oh my gosh she ate her twin!" was the first comment he made. Well... maybe. I had heard stories and watched documentaries about one twin absorbing the other in the womb. It's hard to describe what I was seeing, and it certainly fit the bill. Was this the case here? I will never know, but I wonder, was I was digging through a 99-year-old ball of twin?

Speaking of the dead by Chelsea L. Tolman

I AM THE AUDIENCE

I am sitting at a conference table of dark glossy wood, I am straight-backed, I have my hands clasped in front of me and my legs are crossed. I am patiently waiting, watching, listening. Around the table in other chairs and sitting on couches are family members who have just experienced the death of someone they love. At this moment, I am the audience.

I watch as expressions of confusion, understanding and consideration swim around the faces of the family as we broach the subjects relating to the funeral, the burial, picking out caskets, vaults and all of the many things that they must decide on. Sometimes the death is expected, and I empathize as I observe those with down-turned, dark sunken eyes and hunched shoulders showing complete exhaustion because for weeks, sometimes months they sat next to the dying waiting for this one day, and it has taken its toll on their reserve.

Sometimes the death was unexpected and the shock of it all leaves the family silent and unable to make decisions. Then there are times when the heaviness of everything gets the best and someone ends up in hysterics of crying or anger.

Speaking of the dead by Chelsea L. Tolman

There are young mothers who planned for their baby's birth and are now picking out caskets instead of cradles. Teen brothers and sisters are stuck in shock realizing they have to face their friends at school and explain that a sibling took their own life. And husbands and wives who lost their sweetheart after fifty years together are now faced with learning how to live a life alone.

And I am watching. I am familiar with the facial expressions and the body language and it all tells me a story. It tells me what these people are feeling and who the dead person was to them.

It's not always dark though. There are families that have accepted the place they are in now and prepared for this meeting, giving me accounts of a life lived that was fun and full. I get to hear about the antics pulled by people I never knew, yet closely resemble someone in my own life. Many times I have laughed with a family about the father who was a trickster or grandfather who told them dirty jokes. I can relate to the Grandmothers who always had candy available and would not let you leave her house without a full belly. A mother who built a house with strict rules and only now it is understood that it was all in your best interest and the intent was full of love. Brothers who gave us nicknames and sang silly songs. A sister who after years of fighting over bedroom boundaries, now are willing to share everything together. Life, and death has its place and time. It is in these moments that I revel in my own family dynamics and appreciate the memories.

I get an intimate look at a person that I will never meet. I get to make friends with people that I otherwise would have never known. Family dynamics that I compare to my own family come to life in this room around a conference table of dark glossy wood. It is an honor and it is remembered. So many stories, personal and real and I get to be a part of it. Here, I am the audience.

SPIRITED MORTUARY

    In all the years of being a mortician, I have never seen a ghost, at least I don't think I have. The subject of ghosts can be tricky. Did I see or hear something? Maybe I did, maybe I didn't. Far too often people think that ghosts crowd around the mortuary and set up residency. I believe that if there are such things as ghosts they would be hanging out where they were most comfortable in life, at their home for instance, or their favorite places to vacation, or even where they died. This makes more sense than swarming inside a mortuary, a place that they have probably never visited before, and around people they have never met. There is an argument that ghosts may stay with their body until it's buried, sure, why not? But, wherever a spirit, ghost or haunt ends up, I assure you I do not see them at the mortuary, or do I?

    I lived in an apartment above a small mom and pop mortuary. It was a really big space. There were three bedrooms and two full bathrooms that branched off a long and narrow hallway. There was a huge living room with 1970's faux wood laminate flooring and dirty cream-colored walls. In the living room were huge windows overlooking the parking lot and the garages beyond. There was a small dining room that jutted out of the kitchen area that came complete with olive green appliances and gold specked cream countertops. The kitchen cabinets and cupboards had been painted over so many times that most of the didn't close properly, laden with so many layers of paint. The apartment had plenty of room to share with other people but I had the whole thing to myself, all alone.

There were ghost stories from previous employees who had lived in the apartment. There was supposed to be a small boy, that was mean and a trickster, who lived in the "blue room" (a small room painted the color of deep ocean, it was currently being used for storage). There was also a story of a woman in a white dress that walked up and down the hallway that led to the bedrooms and bathrooms. Bah! I had no concerns that these supposed spirits were fixtures in this space. I do believe that the setting was ripe for these types of experiences though, apartment above a funeral home, dark hallway, dimly lit rooms and dark paint, these things lend to the perception of "otherworldly" things. I imagine the previous residents, who were also all alone during long dark nights, heard the squeaks creeks of an old building in the late hours and let their imagination see things that weren't really there. So, of course I dismissed the stories and settled in to the apartment.

To prove my point that there were no ghosts hanging about, I decided to inspect the blue room, the one I was told to avoid. It was such a dingy place. The overhead light didn't work, so I plugged in a lamp near the back corner that immediately gave off an eerie glow, throwing weird shadows into the angles of the room. Even with the light reflecting off of the walls, it just wasn't enough light to penetrate the deep darkness that hovered in there. Mismatched furniture piled in various places and dusty boxes filled with old invoices and papers painted a scene for the perfect ghost story. The walls had holes from pictures that had hung on them from previous years and dings and scratches from people moving furniture around and not being careful. Dotting the portions of the deep blue painted walls not covered by stacked furniture and boxes were childishly-drawn stick figures in pencil and marker along-side names and dates that were meaningless to me.

I can see where the stories had come from, the dark color, the dinginess, the shadows. It was a creepy room and cold, colder than the rest of the apartment. After spending some time in this room alone, I was satisfied that the stories were unfounded, I turned off the lamp and walked out but kept the door slightly ajar, just to prove that I wasn't afraid. Inky black was all you could see through the slightly opened door (even in the middle of the day, the light simply could not break through the darkness in there) and every time I walked passed the open door, I could feel the cold air seeping out into the hallway. After a few days I made the choice to close the door to keep the cold in and ignore the room all together.

I love cemeteries. I love taking pictures of cemeteries. I cherished looking at the various statues, especially ones that were darkened in places from rain and sun. I collected pictures of headstones that had ironic last names like Grave or Head. One night I decided to start printing these pictures to make room on my camera. I had previously set up my office in the small dining room. On the table I had a computer tower attached to a monitor, not like the monitors we have now but the big heavy monitors that you had to carry with both arms while leaning back to balance the weight. I also had a typewriter, a pile of folders and various papers and a printer.

As the printer warmed up, I loaded the tray with photo paper and then began to transfer my photos from my camera to the computer, placing the ones I wanted to print into a separate folder. The printer was terribly slow at printing so once it had whirred into action, I headed out to the grocery store to avoid the painful wait of watching it produce one agonizing line at a time.

When I got back to the apartment, I walked into the kitchen and saw that my cemetery pictures were scattered about the dining room. Some were left on the tray and were turned around and upside down like someone had picked them up, rifled through them and just dumped them back in the tray. I panicked for a minute like maybe someone was in the apartment. I looked towards the living room, then looked down the hallway but I didn't investigate any further than that, I was confident that no one was there and there was some other reason this happened. I attributed the mess to a gust of wind created when I came home and opened the door from the outside. I knew that this was not really possible though, since the exterior door was down a hall that branched off of the main hallway and much too far from the kitchen for a gust to reach, but that was the only rational explanation I could think of. There was no one that would have come into the apartment, it was late evening, the sun already set making it dark outside. No one bothers a mortuary in the darkness unless you worked there. I started the task of picking up my prints off of the floor and loving the way they turned out, imagining what type of frames I would get and which walls they would hang on. As I was looking them over, I noticed fingerprints? Right along the edges of the papers (front and back!). It was like someone with ink on their fingers had held them and left their prints on the glossy paper. They were undoubtedly fingerprints, the lands and grooves clearly showing where the fingertips had grasped the edges. I had no explanation for this. I really didn't know what to think. I couldn't imagine anyone who would have come in to the apartment just to check out my pictures, and if someone did, why on earth would they scatter the pages and most curious why would their hands have ink on them?! I was baffled.

In my reverie of examining this phenomenon, I absently turned around toward the hallway, papers in hand and looked down the hallway again and there she was. At the very back of the hall was a woman in a white dress. I saw her clearly, she was looking right at me. I froze. As I watched her she slowly she started making her way towards me, not walking really, more like floating. I quickly looked down for one more glance at my fingerprinted papers and when I looked back up, she was gone! She had just vanished. In those few seconds that I saw this woman in white, unmistakably floating towards me, I attributed the fingerprints to something other than human hands. Did she pick up my papers, then scatter them about?

Most people describe the experience of seeing a ghost as scary, disturbing, the air was cold, the adrenaline rushed through their body. Not for me. It was more like she was just curious. Her demeanor wasn't threatening, in fact I wished she would come back. I stood, holding my pictures theorizing about what I had just seen. I still don't have an explanation, I cannot attribute this experience to a sheet hanging from a doorway or over tiredness or lack of food or too much alcohol. I question myself even now, did I really see this woman who looked right at me? How was it that she was even in my apartment, floating down the hallway near the bedroom that I slept in. Still baffled, I shook off the experience and continued to pick up my prints then placed them neatly in a pile on the table. During my time living in that apartment, when the darkness of night had settled over the building, I would occasionally look down the hallway. I never expected to see her again and somehow, I knew that I wouldn't. We had our moment and that was enough.

Speaking of the dead by Chelsea L. Tolman

Sadly, I no longer have these prints, they were lost along with many things during the years of moving and exes. So, are there spirits, ghosts or haunts wandering around in the mortuaries? I have seen no evidence of that, or have I?

Speaking of the dead by Chelsea L. Tolman

OFF CENTER

I have had the honor of being taught by some exceptional embalmers and funeral directors. The knowledge I have gained is exponential in that I have built on what these men have taught me as a mortician. So many factors go into this profession, not just embalming techniques, not just meeting with families, not just perfect placement of the body, cosmetic color, and fleet maintenance. There is this and so much more involved in creating a funeral. In the years that I have been taught and have taught others, I have lost some of these people to death for various reasons and it always hits like a brick. It is not easier, as a funeral director, to lose someone I loved or was important to me. While I have many stories of these dearly departed souls of my past, this story is about the funeral of a mentor who I held in the highest regard.

For a big part of my career in funeral service, I worked under a man who was the director in charge for the firm. It was small and family owned. Good days, bad days, boring days, hyper busy and never eating days, we did it all together. I learned the hard lessons here, little sleep but lots of laughs. This man taught me embalming techniques, the difference between a trust and life insurance, how to park cars and lead a

174

Speaking of the dead by Chelsea L. Tolman

funeral procession, how to grow a garden, paint the parking lot lines, fix plumbing and electrical… you name it, if the funeral home needed it, I was given a lesson on how to repair it or run it.

We spent days talking about life and all its crazy and fine points. We played pranks on each other and like a well-maintained machine we got to where it only took a hand signal or certain look to understand what was happening and what needed to be done. The good, the bad and the ugly was the daily in our routines. I became part of the family inside and outside of work, so, it was an incredibly difficult decision to accept a management position in another state and leave the comfort of what I knew. Moving onward and upward in my career meant leaving behind the quaint life I had built. With so many years of my career ahead of me, I felt the opportunity looming like a mountain begging to be climbed.

Life moved on as it always will, and I often thought of my small-town work family. I visited a few times and got caught up on the town gossip. Every time I went back it was like I had never left. Then, one day I received a call from an old coworker. We talked and caught up on things, then she gave me the news. The man I had worked under for so many years had died! It was totally unexpected, the shock was unreal. He had been in good health and active in life. I had no words.

I made my way back to my old home, the flight was somber, and I almost felt like, when I landed, it was going to turn out to be a huge prank, a joke. It wasn't.

Upon arrival at the mortuary, I didn't know what to expect. After saying hellos and discussing the tragedy that had happened, it was time to see the man in the casket. I walked up to the door of the big viewing room, the casket was already in place, the man dressed and cosmetized. This room was the largest viewing room in the building, it had two big white square pillars, floor to ceiling jutting up through the center, surrounded by a sea of emerald green carpet. On the outskirts of the room were intricate antique end tables with couches and chairs adorned with leaf patterns in maroons and greens perfectly accenting the dark wood of the furniture. I knew this room, I had placed many caskets in this room and I thought I knew what to expect. However, upon approach, the expanse of what was set out before me was like a pit of vipers that I had to navigate. It wasn't that there was a threat – it was the memories and the fact that I just didn't want to be there. So

Speaking of the dead by Chelsea L. Tolman

many people I had placed in here for a viewing, so many flowers I had arranged for the ease of someone else's grief. This day was never supposed to happen, it wasn't supposed to be my grief on display. With deliberate steps and small breaths I made it to the casket, where my mentor lay motionless in his repose. I was just waiting for him to sit up, or blink, or breathe though knowing, with my experience, this was not going to happen.

In my years at this place, I had worked closely with so many wonderful people. These men and women were at the heart of who I had become. So many trials, laughs and struggles that we had all helped each other through and many funerals, so very many funerals. From the administrative staff to the directors and embalmers, this had been my life, learning what it meant to care for others and all the nuances attached to it. During the funeral my old coworkers were a blessed distraction, also coming from other locations. We had all moved on and we had all come back for this. We all had been apprentices to him or others in that funeral home and had moved on to become full-fledged funeral directors. Together we decided, as homage to this great man, that we would all direct his funeral together.

Speaking of the dead by Chelsea L. Tolman

It was an incredible honor to stand beside all of these directors, some of whom I myself had taught, and give our mentor the funeral he deserved. We coordinated everything, it was a show, presenting his legacy of funeral directors as a tribute. As the crowd came in and took their seats in the chapel, the reality sank in deeper. We all worked in concert like hundreds of previous funerals in this place. I was given the task of helping to roll the casket to the front of the chapel and then, all of us together, walked down the center aisle to the back of the chapel and turned around to check our work, like we always did. Only to see that the casket was off center!

This was one of the pet peeves of our mentor. Even through our horror we chuckled at the faux pa. He would be lecturing us at this moment "You had one job!" Such careful planning, so in sync we were. The tiny details were handled without flaw, and then we screwed up the crucial placement of the casket! No one outside of the industry would ever notice there was a problem, but every funeral director for miles around would scream at the incredulity of an off-center casket! And I was a part of it. I did it. So, of course, we ran to the lobby and laughed our asses off! It was a great send-off to screw up the focal point of the whole funeral and then we shed a tear that we were sending off the man who we had worked with for so many years. It was truly bitter-sweet.

There was a period of open mic (where anyone in the crowd can stand up and say something) and most of us directors, including me, shared our story. I talked about how my experience was learning more than from this man than rolling a casket into a chapel. At the end of the funeral the crowd dispersed, we said our goodbyes and as people left I knew that I would not see them again, my life had moved on and away from this place.

There would not be a burial, our next destination was the crematory. So, I and a long-time coworker and friend volunteered for the job. We took the body of a man so revered out of the oak wood rental casket and laid him on a wheeled cot to place him in the small transport hearse for his final ride like we had done so many times before, but always with people we didn't know.

The crematory was located in an industrial section of the town. A large garage surrounded by other large garages and big warehouses. My coworker backed the hearse up to the large open door and we were greeted by the crematory operator. He had everything ready to go. The space was dusty from the door being opened and closed so many times throughout the day. There were stacks of coffin-sized cardboard boxes (required for a body to be in to be cremated) to our left and the retort (the machine used for cremation) was to the right. We gently placed my mentor's body into a cardboard box. The retort and already been started in preparation and we stayed until the process began, then got in the hearse and drove away. The end to a life of a man who left a legacy and changed my life forever.

SON OF A PREACHER MAN

The funeral home was fluttering with people, filling the hallways and lobby with chatter and the occasional burst of laughter. The staff was buzzing about, moving flowers and parking cars. We were all getting ready for a funeral, and I was the funeral director. In this town it was customary for the officiating clergy to show up to the mortuary about thirty minutes before the funeral was scheduled to start. They would talk with the family briefly, then come into the office and give the director the "order of service" (who was speaking when, what song was to play and how the service would end) this was the normal routine. On this day though, it was starting to get uncomfortably close to service time and I had not yet seen the preacher. I decided to call the number I had in the file only to be greeted by a voicemail. I spoke with the family of the deceased about the situation and luckily someone had the phone number for the preacher's son, so they gave him a call. The son was just as baffled as we were and said he would try and find his father and give us an update as soon as he had one.

It is important to start a funeral on time for a number of reasons. The guests who attend usually have scheduled their day to be available for a certain amount of time, the musicians may have other appointments to get to once their part of the service is over with, the police escort is counting on us to leave the funeral home within a given timeframe so they can return to their duties, the cemetery crew will be waiting and ready with their equipment based on the start time of the funeral and of course, the funeral home may have another service later, other families to meet with or embalmings to perform. So, starting a funeral on time is incredibly important to everyone involved.

With no word from the son yet, I went to inform the crowd as to what was happening. I calmly walked into the visitation room full of people and announced that we were waiting on the preacher still and that the service would be starting late. I then made my way to the chapel, where some people were already seated, and made the same announcement from the pulpit. Then, I waited, and prepared to conduct the service myself in case the preacher never showed.

Finally, minutes before the start time, I received a call from the son, he informed me that his father had gotten lost on the way to the funeral home. He said his father had been showing signs of dementia recently and this type of thing was happening more and more. He told me his father was insistent on officiating the service, even though I had offered to handle it and they were just around the corner. When they arrived, I made my way out to the front porch to greet them. The porch floor was a red stained concrete bordered by a red brick building on one side and large white columns and bright full flower beds on the other side. It led out to the parking lot where I could see the pair making their way towards me. The preacher was elderly, very tall, bone thin and barely able to make full steps. He shuffled along in a dark brown suit hanging loosely off his shoulders and around his arms and legs, his white hair was slicked back from his ears and he firmly clutched his tattered bible to his chest with one arm. Close behind was his son, patiently helping him along. I walked up to the preacher and greeting him with my arm held out for a handshake, only to have him veer aside slightly, eyes frantic and focused on getting inside, and walked right past me like I was just an obstacle to get around. I stood there, standing with my hand held out to the air, leaving it there to shake the son's hand instead.

The son apologized for his dad and I told him that I realized that his dad was confused and understandably embarrassed and not to give it another thought. Once we were inside the building, I made another attempt at a conversation with the preacher by asking about the order of service, and we successfully pieced together a program for the funeral. After a short prayer with the family, we were finally ready to make our way to the chapel. The son escorted his father right up to the chapel doors and then stopped to wait in the hallway, feeling uncomfortable in his jeans and t-shirt, having just rushed out of the middle of a workday. A coworker and I were pushing the casket right behind them and the family followed close behind us.

The chapel had a large stage where the pulpit sat. Behind the pulpit was low bench that provided seating for the clergy and other speakers. On the back wall of the stage hung a huge cream-colored curtain which served as a backdrop for flowers sent to the family which, when well placed, created bursts of color and texture.

As we entered the chapel through a side door, just to the left was a glossy black baby grand piano that sat in front of a set of wide steps leading up to the stage, to the right were the rows of pews full of friends of the deceased and straight ahead was the space between the pews and stage where we would be centering the casket.

Speaking of the dead by Chelsea L. Tolman

Once we had the casket placed, I directed the staff to seat the family and then rushed over to the stairs by the piano to offer my arm as assistance to steady the preacher who was clearly struggling to get up the steps. The man looked back at me with slight sneer and offered a weak growl and I understood that his pride was shaken enough already. With a chapel full of people watching, I had no intention of embarrassing him any further, so I stepped back a bit but remained ready if he stumbled. One shaky leg at a time found a step and after a few tense moments (tense for me anyway) he made it to the top and shuffled over to the pulpit.

The staff and I left the chapel and I went to find the son and see how he was holding up. He informed me that he had a conversation with his mother and that he would be taking his father home right after the service, they would not be joining us at the cemetery. I agreed this was wise, as his father was obviously upset and exhausted from his ordeal of being lost.

When the funeral was over, I calmly walked back near the steps to the stage, feigning the need to do something important while side-glancing and staying as close as possible in the event the preacher toppled or slipped. He shuffled and hobbled and grunted but made it to the bottom of the stairs safely and on his own. Right at that moment the son walked over and took his father by the arm to lead him away. The preacher promptly threw a fit totally unbefitting a revered clergy man! He raised his voice, stating he was absolutely going to the cemetery. It was his right! His face was beet red and his fist not clutching his bible was balled up like a two-year-old in a tantrum. I acted quickly and showed the son the back way out of the chapel so he wouldn't have to drag his shouting father through the crowd. As I held the back door for them, the son gave a heavy sigh and pulled the preacher away slowly with a mournful backward glance, looking like a whipped puppy. With a heavy heart for the poor son, I made my way back to the chapel and escorted the casket to the hearse and the crowd to their waiting cars and off we went to the cemetery.

I received a call from the preacher's son the next day, he informed me that his father would not be available for funerals from that point on. He sounded broken and exhausted. I imagined how hard it would it be to force an adored and respected parent into retirement. It was a humble moment, a sad day that this man, once strong and proud, couldn't remember how to get to a place he had been to hundreds of times and his son was now laden with a new set of responsibilities as their roles inevitably reversed.

Speaking of the dead by Chelsea L. Tolman

THE END OF A RAINBOW

I was fourteen years old when my family moved from Utah to Nevada. It wasn't an easy transition. A small town Utah girl thrown into "Sin City!" I was finding it difficult to fit in anywhere and then I discovered a friend living two doors down from my new house. She was the best! A blonde beauty with porcelain skin, long legs and tiny feet. We clicked right away and as most teens did in Las Vegas, we got into a *lot* of trouble! We spent hours lying on my trampoline. We would slather baby oil over our skin and spritz lemon juice in our hair looking for the perfect beach ready look. We borrowed each other's clothes and sang and danced in my bedroom to Depeche Mode or Erasure until we fell to the floor laughing.

I knew she was sick, but she rarely showed it. She had a vertical scar on her belly from where she told me the doctors had taken out a section of her intestines leaving her with a belly bulge she was always self-conscious about. She would get tired and need to rest from time to time, yet, she never complained. She was always laughing, smiling and loving. Right out of high school she met a man whom she married and her greatest wish was to have a child, yet, with her illness this was risky for her poor, damaged body. But she was determined, and no amount of warning or pleading was going to stop her. And then, she got pregnant.

I took on the task of looking after her during the day. I would go over to her apartment to help out, making sure she was resting and eating. Being adventurous spirits, we decided to start a business making ice cream pies. We were certain that the ice cream pie business was going to make us millions! We tried every which way we could think of to make a working recipe and with every failed attempt to bake a crispy, flaky crust and a firm ice cream filling, we would try a different way the next day. We made fantastic messes, we flung flour and sugar and lots and lots of ice cream in every nook and cranny of her cramped apartment kitchen. I miss those days. The music blaring and flour covered ice cream bits flying, we always had a blast.

One day, I walked into her apartment only to be met with a strange silence. I called for her and then noticed the bathroom door was closed. So, I went to the kitchen and started to unpack the flour, ice cream and fruit choices that we would attempt that day and then waited. When she finally came out of the bathroom, her face was beaded from perspiration. Her blonde, shoulder length hair hung in strands from sweat and her porcelain doll face marred with dark rimmed and bloodshot eyes. She wore a grey cotton, thigh

189

length nightgown blemished with wetness and creased folds from hard restless sleep and she could hardly walk on her own. She stumbled forward only barely grabbing the frame of the bathroom door to stop her fall. I dropped what I was doing and ran to assist her to the couch then gently helped her lie down. I pulled a patchwork blanket over her all the way up to her chin. She was looking up at me with silent tears streaming down her cheeks, then explained that she had miscarried the night before. I said nothing, I gently crawled onto the couch beside her, cradled her head in my lap and lightly stroked her hair. We sat like that in silence for hours.

My friend finally rallied from the blow and our daily adventures of making ice cream pies became the norm again. This time I would make her sit in a chair in the kitchen next to me. She was the foreman and I took her instructions on what to try next. Her husband would come home every day and shake his head at the soggy pie crusts dripping with melted ice cream and the both of us covered in flour and fruit and always, we had the radio blasting.

After the incident, I had taken her husband aside and warned him to let her body heal before they tried to get pregnant again. I threatened some sort of bodily harm should he not assure that she had enough time to heal. He promised me that he would.

Speaking of the dead by Chelsea L. Tolman

I will always remember the last day that I spent with my friend. It had been about a couple of months since her miscarriage and we were sitting on her couch. Suddenly she turned to me with a huge grin sprouting on her face. She was silent for a moment and then said. "I am glad you are here for this". I had no idea what she was talking about. She sprang up off of the couch and grabbed my hand pulling me to her tiny apartment bathroom. She bent down, rummaged through the counter under the sink and pulled out a small brown paper bag. Then silently, still smiling, she handed me the bag. I opened the bag and looked inside, and my heart skipped in shock. It was a pregnancy test. I felt sick. I needed to throw up. She might be pregnant again?!

Her body was still so weak. I only paused for a moment before giving her my best smile then pulled the pregnancy test out of the bag to set on the bathroom counter. She immediately grabbed the box and tore it open like a child with a Christmas present, my dread deepening but knowing she needed me cheerful and supportive for this moment. I started to walk out of the bathroom when she said "No, stay. I want you here for this". So, I stayed while she peed into the cup. She smiled up at me like an angel, glowing with hope. I could barely stand the effort not to burst into tears and run away. Her anxiousness and my trepidation made for a palpable sense of confusion for me as we waited for the fluid to soak long enough to give the answer of "yes" or "no" and it didn't take long. Bright and blaring, this plastic stick confirmed my fear and her deepest wishes, she was pregnant, again!

I don't know how I was able to cheer and jump up and down with her, our arms wrapped around each other. My head was swimming and my legs were numb, but I did it, and she was beautiful in her full smile and girlish giggling.

We picked up her husband from work that evening. She drove their big white ford truck and I sat in the back seat, fuming and silent and sad. As her husband started to get into the passenger seat he was greeted with the plastic stick staring at him from the dash. I could not see his face from the back seat, but I noticed his body freeze like someone hit the pause button for a flash of a second. He pulled himself into the truck the rest of the way and she wrapped her arms around his neck, kissing his face in every crease with fresh silent tears running down her cheeks. He reacted how he was expected to. She finished accosting him and he slumped back into his seat. I reached through the belt side of the passenger seat grabbed as much of his skin as I could and pinched his arm, hard! I twisted and squeezed his skin until I was sure I left a nasty bruise and hoping I drew some blood! He didn't react, he didn't turn around and he didn't say a word to me when they dropped me off at my house. I got out and closed the door behind me, finally letting my own silent tears run down my cheeks as I walked.

The next day when I got to my friends' door, and to my surprise, found it locked? I knocked and waited. I knocked again and waited. The blinds were closed, the windows were dark. Panic was setting in. I called, no answer. I called again, no answer. I then called her mother and got the news. My friend had been rushed to the hospital and she was refusing to see anyone, even me.

Over the next few days, I was told repeatedly that she did not want to see me. I spoke to her mother and her husband to get updates, learning that she had miscarried again and had sunk into a deep depression. As soon as I knew she was home, I stopped by once again. She wouldn't answer the door or the phone. Knowing that depression is not rational, and she needed time to mourn I left her alone to contact me when she felt ready, but she never did.

Over the next couple of years, I never heard from her. I tried to contact her, only to be met with silence. The next phone call I received regarding my friend, was the news of her death. I was told when and where the funeral was to be and in

Speaking of the dead by Chelsea L. Tolman

that phone call I learned that she had given birth a son! She
had the child she had always wanted, and it cost her life.
Numb to the core, I rode in the passenger seat of the car, a
dear companion whom I had grown close to over the last years
driving me. I don't remember the trip there, only that it was in
a small dusty town some ways from the city.

Together we walked into the chapel. The place was
packed with people and we got in the long line of people that
snaked through the room. It was almost our turn at the casket
when we approached my friends' mother. She grabbed me and
squeezed me so tight that I thought I would burst! We held
each other for a moment. I learned from her that my friend
would be cremated and when I asked after her son she told me
he wasn't there and that I could see him knowing that I would
not, that I could not.

I approached the casket. Her blonde hair was atop her
head fashioned in perfect golden ringlets. She looked so
peaceful, so innocent. I reached out and placed my hand on
top of hers, then wrapped my fingers around her fingers. Even
with mortuary makeup her hands and arms were covered in
dark bruises from needles injecting whatever chemicals the
doctors thought she needed. Eventually my companion pulled
me away as I was holding up the line. I was overwhelmed
with a gripping ache that my friend was gone. She had pushed

194

me away without any explanation. I was not a part of her son's birth and I missed her, and I hated that I missed her.

One of my friend's favorite pastimes was chasing rainbows. Together we had driven all over the city hunting the elusive arcs of color always to watch them slowly disappear before we could reach its origin. She had told me that one day she was going to catch the end of a rainbow and find its pot of gold. I loved living in her world of optimism. Thinking that if you wish hard enough that something as intangible as a rainbow could be captured. I believed with her in a fanciful way that there was a pot of gold and a friendly leprechaun just waiting for someone determined enough to find them.

The service over, my companion and I were on the two-lane road headed home. On both sides of the road were long expanses of dirt, rocks and grasses. Then suddenly over the road ahead of us was a rainbow beginning to form. Knowing me well, having heard all the stories I had told of my friend's quest, she pulled the car over and stopped on the side of the road. We watched as the rainbow continued to form. It was bright and arched from one side of the road to the other and on both sides of the road you could clearly see where the rainbow ended. And it was so close! I felt if I walked towards it for just a minute I would reach it, find the leprechaun and be given the pot of gold.

Speaking of the dead by Chelsea L. Tolman

We sat in silence as the rainbow formed and then start to fade. The perfect homage to my friend's death. From beginning to end and all the beautiful colors in between, we witnessed the beginning and the end of a rainbow.

Speaking of the dead by Chelsea L. Tolman

<u>COLOR IS BLIND</u>

I had just started my shift when my boss approached me saying he had a challenge and wanted to know if I was up for it. Not asking what the challenge was I readily agreed, being ambitious and young. He led me to the back room and showed me a woman lying on a table who had been embalmed the night before, and she was green, lime green!

You may have heard the term jaundice before, if you haven't it is when there is an over accumulation of a substance called bilirubin (yellow pigment) in the blood. It turns the tissue of the person yellow, skin, eyes, you get the picture. This is a challenge for an embalmer. The chemical reaction when introduced to formaldehyde (an agent in embalming fluid) is that it turns the tissues green. There are chemicals made just for this and tricks to prevent this from happening but the person who had embalmed this woman did not use caution and went ahead with a full-strength formaldehyde mixture. Which turned her skin green.

My boss asked if I could possibly cover her with cosmetics well enough to have a public viewing. I was totally up for the challenge and quite excited to flex my still unrefined skills and told him I could handle it. In these cases, aside from the color, the skin sometimes stays quite malleable instead of firming like it should during embalming, making it difficult to apply makeup. So, I pulled out my arsenal of creams and powders and got to work. After mixing colors and applying them, then removing and mixing more colors I got to a point where I felt the woman was presentable enough for the public, she looked like she spent weeks in the sun but her face was no longer green.

It was after hours at this point and I was cleaning up to go home when I was contacted by the funeral homes answering service and given the message to call the woman's daughter right away. I walked to the front office and dialed the number, I am not even sure if it rang on my end when a woman answered, not even saying hello she asked, "Is this the mortuary?" I told her it was. "Okay good" she continued "I forgot to tell the man earlier that you cannot put any makeup on my mother". Trying to be sensitive I explained that there was a challenge with the type of illness her mother had and that she had turned a different color. I also explained that I had successfully covered this unnatural color with a much more natural tone. "Oh no!'" she said frantically "You have to take it off, all of it! Right now!" I was stunned to silence which worked out because she continued. "My mother never wore makeup and she cannot have on even a little bit of makeup". I calmly said I understood, and then more gently explained her mother's condition and her color. Immediately she got angry telling me she knew her mother's condition and it didn't matter and to take the makeup off right now. Actually, it was more like "Put me on hold and go take the makeup off and come back to tell me when you are done!" I tried once more to describe the deep green color that it would be shocking and traumatizing to her and her guests at the viewing then suggested that she come and see for herself before we went so far as to remove the makeup. "I don't care, if you don't take that makeup off right now, God will not recognize her, and she will be wandering lost for eternity".

I had no argument for that, no rebuttal, no response. So, I assured her that when I hung up the phone with her I would go take the makeup off and then call her back once I was finished. I cannot judge a person's beliefs but as I wiped off all of my hard work and revealed the woman's Hulk green skin, I couldn't help but whisper to this dead woman "I hope God recognizes you green"

The viewing was a disaster, people were talking. One woman came to the front desk and berated the funeral home for showing the woman to the public. As for the daughter, she was happy and calm. Even with the guests upset she stood at her mother's casket and beckoned people over, exclaiming

Speaking of the dead by Chelsea L. Tolman

just how beautiful she looked like nothing was out of the ordinary and her mother wasn't the color of limes.

NEVER WAKE THE DEAD

Most people have a routine when first coming to work in the morning. Start the coffee maker, transfer the phones, fire up the computer. My routine at this one particular funeral home was to walk through the back entrance, enter the embalming room and look at the deceased who had been received throughout the night. At this firm it was customary, after embalming, to place the body on a portable table and drape a sheet over them from head to toe. As I walked up to each table, I would pull back the sheets one by one, look at their faces, stroke a head or pat an arm, then cover them back up. It was comforting getting to know each of these people who in the coming days would be dressed, cosmetized, casketed and funeralized. In these moments, I learned their names, had small one-sided conversations with them and hoped things would go smoothly for their families' sake. If there were people that I myself had gone to receive during the witching hour, it made it even more personal. It was important to me to know them and have a sense of them before the families came in to make arrangements.

One morning, I made my way to the embalming room, like always, and started pulling back sheets to say my hello's.

201

Speaking of the dead by Chelsea L. Tolman

I pulled a particular sheet back, and suddenly, the body sat straight up into a sitting position and the person shouted "Good morning!"

OK, breathe...a...minute...and as the adrenaline rushed through my veins, I recognized my coworker laughing hysterically at me from his sitting position on the table. Mind you we kept a clean and tidy house there, but all I could think was "Gross!"

So, for those of you who are not intimately familiar with the dead, they do not sit up, they do not breathe, or blink, or yell "Good Morning". What they do is lie on a table and wait for someone to move them. They may moan a little as the air trapped air in their lungs escapes through their lips, or maybe give a tiny sigh but short of a real zombie apocalypse, the dead do not move on their own, or yell words, or wake up. I know disappointing huh? However, that is the way it is.

So, back to silly coworkers scaring me almost to death. I myself have never lain on a table just to scare a coworker and this was the first in a string of pop up sheets until I learned to look for signs of life and play a trick of my own, a little cold water anyone?!

Speaking of the dead by Chelsea L. Tolman

THE TERRIBLE, HILARIOUS FALL

In all of my years as a small female funeral director, I can tout many times that I have moved a deceased body from strange and compromising situations, with assistance or on my own. Upstairs, downstairs, through narrow hallways, sliding in mud and slipping on ice, struggling to move ungiving weight from tangled, cotton bedsheets. I have always found a way though, never faltered, strained terribly, but always got the job done without injury to myself or the person I was charged with keeping safe. I have been applauded that my small frame held a remarkably strong and careful woman who has expertly handled herself in situations that defied the laws of what is first assumed to be, my nature.

We received a call one day, it was an expected death, nothing out of the ordinary for a mortuary. A coworker and I drove to the address we were given. It was an apartment building, and we were instructed to go to the third floor where the deceased was located. I entered first to meet the family and make a plan of how to successfully transfer the person from the bed to our cot, through the apartment and then down the three flights to our waiting van. I surveyed the setting and noted all of the obstacles that we would need to negotiate, couches, end tables, lamps. With no elevator close, our best way down with the cot were the stairs, they were steep and concrete and narrow and would be difficult to maneuver but nothing more treacherous or challenging than anything I had handled before. I retrieved my coworker and we started the process of moving the woman into our care. We carefully wrapped her in a clean sheet and then gently slid her onto our cot. We gave the family a precious moment before heading towards the narrow, hardened concrete stairwell.

The woman was survived by a sister who wanted to be present for the process. This is something we usually don't discourage, as it is a family members' right to help in moving someone they love. However, it can be cumbersome however, when a new set of hands start disrupting what the professionals know to work better. We explained to the sister how narrow the stairwell was and it would be safer if we did the job on our own and she could meet us in the parking lot to help at that end. She thankfully agreed, and we entered the concrete maw of the evil snaky stairwell.

Anyone who has moved furniture down a flight of stairs can understand the push-me, pull-you Tango dance it requires to get down the steps with the furniture and your limbs intact and uninjured. This is the struggle we faced at this moment. My coworker was ahead of me and setting the pace, which was faster than my cautious strides could bear while carrying my end of the load. "Take it slow", "Don't rush", "You're going to fast", "Slow down!" were my cries as the serpentine stairwell gulped us down it's throat. We were getting to our destination when suddenly the momentum and my guarded steps went out of sync and right then, without warning, my coworker stopped to round the bend of the next landing jarring my already rickety footwork and strained handhold of the cot handle. Before I knew it, my grasp failed completely! The handle I had been holding turned into an arm of steel claws and wrenched it's bolts down my shin only stopping to pin my foot to the stair step I was currently standing on. This all happened so abruptly that I completely lost my balance. My quick reflexes grabbed at the hand railing, I missed it by millimeters and I pitched forward face-first without my hands to break the fall, awkwardly landing right on top of the dead woman!

My foot pinned, my shin in tatters and my pride shredded and throbbing like the nerves in my leg. I was given a minute of respite before I heard the question "Are you okay?" "Do I look like I am okay damnit!?" Was the screamy response my brain shouted inside my head, but of course, the situation called for something more professional. So, I quickly stood up, laughed it off, gulped my pride and blinked back the haze filming my eyes, grabbed my end of the cot and continued to hobble and strain down the rest of the staircase to the waiting sister and our van.

Refusing to look down at what I imagined to be a blood soaked and tattered pant leg, I left my coworker to get the cot loaded by himself while I tried not to limp or wince, creating a fantastic, straight backed, hopefully professional demeanor, while hugging the woman goodbye and reassuring her that her sister was in good hands.

With stoic pride and elegance, I pulled myself into the passenger side of the van and kept smiling while waving goodbye to the woman who, thankfully, had no idea about the incident that had just occurred. As soon as we were on the road I pulled up my pantleg which was somehow undamaged. It seemed that my stocking had worked as an absorbent, holding in place tiny droplets of now dried blood. As I carefully peeled the stocking down inch by agonizing inch, it pulled off a dried bead that sprang forth fresh bright crimson drops to trickle down the scraped skin and quickly bruising wound on my shin. I hadn't decided how to handle the situation yet, so I didn't say much in the way of words just suddenly gave out a crazy, maniacal laugh as I imagined myself folded over, inadvertently kissing the belly of an occupied cot with my foot stuck under its handle. I couldn't stop laughing yet, inside my head was a tear streaked sobbing mess of a girl, not knowing whether I was ever going to walk normally again. I think this feeling is what people refer to when announcing that someone has cracked! We arrived back at the funeral home. Walking was just as difficult as I had imagined, and of course the rendition of my superb comedic performance had to be told and then repeated over again. Oh, the woes of the grotesquely injured.

It took almost two months for the goose eggs, yes eggs! to stop throbbing with every step. And every time I took a minute to change the dressing of my injury and relive the day that I toppled over a dead woman, I made sure my coworker saw at it as well, laughing again at the image of me tipped over uncomfortably and hopefully reminding him that the seconds he may have saved by being impatient had caused weeks of agony for me.

Speaking of the dead by Chelsea L. Tolman

BRICK HOUSE

As a funeral director apprentice, I faced many challenges with being a female. What made it even more difficult was that I am a small-statured female. In my college days it was almost impossible to get a job a funeral home to be a funeral director. I was relentless though. I sent my resume to local funeral homes, then made follow-up calls every day after classes. I would show up in the lobbys asking for the hiring managers explaining why they should give me a job, any job, that would open my career path to be a funeral director.

Even after all of my efforts it still took a fellow student and a helping hand from inside the mortuary to finally get hired on as a funeral assistant. Even still I had to prove that I could handle every task that was required for the position and not only that I could just do the job either, in some instances it felt like I had to prove I could do it better. Many times, I would show up at a hospital pushing a cot only to be met by a security guard who would let me in the morgue and then stand in the corner, arms crossed, just waiting for me to fail or ask for help. However, my male counterparts got jovial, friendly security guards happily pulling on gloves and would help them move the body from the morgue table to the cot. This unbalanced reaction of people between a male and female funeral director was almost always present. The sentiment being that girls were supposed to answer phones and type letters, not move dead bodies.

One of the first times I went on a house call (when we pick up a deceased person from their home) I was with another director. House calls always require two people. Unlike hospitals with wide hallways and elevators, designed for the breadth of a cot and large rooms with space for multiple people moving about, houses more times than not have small bedrooms located down narrow corridors with slender doorways and almost always stairs. One person cannot reasonably be expected to negotiate these obstacles alone.

The director I was with that night had never been worked with me before so neither of us knew what to expect from each other. He had gone into the house by himself first to meet the family and make a plan for moving the deceased gentleman. I waited in the hearse for him to come back out and give me the signal that the family was ready. This was the normal procedure for a house call. It is simpler for one person to go inside the house first, meet with the family and give them information. Then when it is time to leave come out and get the second person to take the cot inside and transfer the body to our cot and out to the hearse. So, I waited in the car while he went inside.

I saw the director walk out of the house, making his way towards me. This was my signal so I jumped into action. I got out of the car and made my way to the back of the hearse to start removing the cot but as he approached he asked me to stop and wait. He said the gentleman was in the very back bedroom of a narrow hallway and then he stated that it was much too difficult for me to handle and that he was going to call someone else to come and help. Feeling annoyed about having my ability dismissed so quickly, I asked if I could go inside and see for myself whether or not I could handle the task. After some hesitation, he agreed.

The bedroom was a straight shot down a hallway from the living room, but our medical cot was too long to make the tight turn at the end of the hallway into the into the bedroom itself. This meant the man had to be hand carried from the bed to the cot, which we would have to leave in the hallway. The man was taller than average yet bone thin meaning he would be easier to hand-carry. The hallway was narrow and quite compromising due to the myriad of framed pictures poking from the walls on both sides of the hall. Having been in similar situations before I knew I could handle this. I told the director not to call for additional help, that I was capable of doing my part. Reluctantly he said he would let me try but as soon as it proved to be too much for me, he was going to make that call.

We wheeled the cot to the end of the hallway right in front of the bedroom door. Then we entered the room and started preparing the man to move him. Carefully we rolled him side to side to gently pushing a fresh sheet underneath him. Once he was securely wrapped in the sheet we both lifted him up in our arms and sidled towards the door. This required some negotiating, turning of his legs and edging through the narrow doorway to allow the director and me to squeeze through as well. We both grunted and strained but made it through the doorway to finally lay the man onto the waiting cot.

This however, was only the first hurdle. The doorway out of the house had a small wooden porch with high railings on all sides except for a short set of stairs led down to the front yard. With the cot being so long, we had to lift it straight up over one side of the railing and then turn it as we maneuvered out of the front doorway, which then gave us just enough room to set the cot down onto the porch in front of the six or seven stairs leading to the sidewalk and waiting hearse. It is a literal lift and strain holding your arms as high as you can reach while moving in compromising positions kind of task. Every thirty seconds or so the director asked how I was doing like he expected me to give up at any moment. To his surprise we got the cot into the hearse, said goodbye to the family and drove away. Once we were on the road the director looked at me and said, "You are strong." I told him thank you. There was silence for a moment and then he said, "No, I mean you are really strong. From now on I will call you Brick House, just like the song."

Speaking of the dead by Chelsea L. Tolman

SIDE BY SIDE

I was informed of a husband and wife who were killed together in a car accident and our mortuary got the call. The couple had gone for a drive. Maybe they were going to the grocery store, maybe to see a movie, I didn't know the details. What I did know was that somehow, they didn't or couldn't stop their car fast enough while driving behind a semi-truck. As a result, they ended up underneath the back end of the rig, ultimately shearing off the top of their car. Neither of them survived.

This would be my first opportunity to see, in real life and on the job, the destruction that motor vehicle accidents can have on a body and on their surviving family members. I remember the words of the director that I was working with. He explained that I was welcome to observe the couple, but I didn't have to, there would always be others. He warned me that both bodies had been greatly damaged from the accident and this could be just too much for a young funeral assistant in the beginning days on the job. I hesitated for only a second before I assured him that I wanted this experience now. I felt this was like a rite of passage, preparing me for my career ahead. With a small nod he turned and beckoned me to follow.

Speaking of the dead by Chelsea L. Tolman

I followed the funeral director down the long hallway in the back of the mortuary toward the garage where the couple lay waiting. The team that went to receive the husband and wife had only just gotten back and while they had removed them from the transport vehicle, they not yet been taken the pair inside the building. As we walked I couldn't help but imagine what this would look like. In my young mind, influenced by TV shows and movies, I imagined the worst scenario possible. I had no idea what an accident this bad really did to a body and no real-life experience to compare it to.

The director opened the door to immediately reveal two cots sitting side-by-side, lying on each was an occupant enclosed in a thick black body bag, like the ones you see in crime TV shows. Surrounding the couple against the walls of the space were shelves that accompany any funeral homes garage. Ledges lined with boxes holding signs, water, towels and décor for the seasons. A tool box caught my eye reminding me of the things we were constantly fixing around the funeral home like loose door knobs and loose toilet handles. In the center of the garage stood a body lift (a device designed to assist lifting the deceased from tables into caskets). The room smelled slightly of exhaust fumes from the cars recently driven. The hearse and the flower van were parked on the opposite side of the room, silently witnessing what happens to people when vehicles are not driven carefully.

The image of the cots alone was enough to invoke just how tragic the situation was. Side-by-side they married each other, side-by-side they raised children together and side-by-side they got into their car that day. Now, side-by-side they lay on cots in the garage of a mortuary.

We walked to the cot closest to us and the director carefully unzipped the thick bag while I stood a few steps away. I slowly stepped closer to see the man lying inside, looking for blood and tissue and gruesome accident things. There was no way to identify him through facial features. The man was wearing dark blue jeans and a shirt of red and blue plaid, all of which were soiled. Scattered about his head and what was visible of his clothing were bits of road debris, glass and shards of broken car pieces. He looked like he had been created out of wax and cosmetics like a movie prop for a horror film, he just didn't look real. What hit me first though was his wallet, lying on his belly it was encased in a sealed plastic bag that had biohazard printed in red over the top. It probably held his driver's license, credit cards, and memberships passes, never to be used again. There was a handful of change that I imagined, like most men he kept in his pocket and jingled absently while standing in conversation, a set of keys that at one time resided in a bowl on the counter in their home or hung on a hook next to the door, patiently waiting for the next drive to the grocery store. In that moment my heart sank as I realized that his children had just lost both of their parents, without warning and without getting to say goodbye.

Years after this experience, I bought a house in a small town in the South that reminded me of this couple. The house had been owned by a husband and wife who had also died in a car accident together. The children they left behind did all they could to get through their pain and loss yet ultimately could not bring themselves to clear out the house that they grew up in. It was just too painful. On my first walkthrough, it looked just like someone had left unexpectedly and never came back. Tiny house shoes sat next to the door patiently waiting their owners return. A shelf of cookbooks in the kitchen held instructions for meals and treats for family gatherings. Each room had its own tale of previous use. A sewing machine whispered that there was hemming left undone, closets full of clothes never again to be worn by their intended owner. The house had sat empty of life long enough for the cobwebs and moisture of the South to take up residence. The air was thick and moldy, and it was dim due to lack of electricity, the only light was what came through the windows which were covered in cobwebs and dust. So naturally, my thoughts went to this first couple I had experienced accidental death with. Lying next to each other on cots in black body bags surrounded by garage things, nestled amongst their belongings that they had taken with them that day and their children who were left with a only a house full of memories.

Tragedy is a necessary part of this job. When people ask me questions of how I handle these situations every day, my mind almost always drifts to this couple. The children were never going to see their parents again. They had to trust the doctor that their parents were dead, they had to trust that the funeral director had the right bodies and they had to deal with other family members, friends and a lifetime of remembrances that they were not yet ready to dismantle and sell to a stranger. So, it shouldn't be how I could handle these things, the question should be how could I not? The families who survive the death of a loved one, always have it worse than I.

I was not involved in making the arrangements for this couple, but I was present when they were laid to rest. It was a chilly fall day and we were surrounded by huge trees half covered in orange and red leaves that dotted the cemetery beyond our blue funeral tent signifying the end of one season and preparing for the next. Surrounded by their children this husband and wife, just like they did in life, will for all eternity be side-by-side.

Speaking of the dead by Chelsea L. Tolman

CREMATION BY PYRE

It was a four-hour drive from Denver, CO to my destination. In all the years I have been in death care, I never imagined that this would be possible. A funeral pyre, out in the open air! Family and friends witnessing the burning of a body, legally?! I turned on to a small dirt road in the middle of nowhere, marked only by a small white sign with the single word "Pyre" painted in red. Waiting for me at the beginning of this dirt road was Stephanie Gaines in her gunmetal Volvo, she has agreed to show me around and explain how this whole thing was made possible.

After greeting each other with a hug, we got back in our cars and I followed her about half a mile up the road to the pyre site. It was all open land scattered with dry brush and weeds choking the desert from all sides. This made me question how a six-foot tall open flame fire would be safe out here. We parked and got out of our cars. To my left were two wooden pillars that marked the start of a dirt trail with various sized rocks lining both sides and the trail ending at a ring of expertly crafted dark brown bamboo fencing. To the side of the pillars stood a wooden structure similar to what you would see at the beginning of a state park trail detailing the hikes available for that area. Instead it held a large bell and, on the walls, hung a handcrafted tree of life in copper sheeting and a sign explaining the sacredness of this place.

Stephanie started our journey by explaining that on the morning of a cremation, friends and neighbors of the deceased would first gather at the pillars and then line the dirt walkway that led to the circled fencing beyond. When the body arrived, usually driven by family members in their personal vans or trucks and the bell was rung three times. The sound of the bell was not a deep gong and not a tinny ring but somewhere in between, something else. Stephanie rang the bell and it reverberated through the desert around us seeming to create an air of calm as the sound echoed away. She continued explaining the process. The pall bearers would carry the body, wrapped in a shroud on a handmade wooden stretcher up the center of the dirt road. Each stretcher was made just for the decease that lay upon it and was designed to fit inside the pyre perfectly.

I imagined this process as we walked and talked, people gathered in silence and lined along the sides of the road in honor of the deceased. The stretcher being lovingly hand carried. I had seen pictures on the internet of this place but being here, feeling a breeze surround me and imagining

221

this gentle and natural process took it to a whole other level, it felt so normal.

The beginning of the funeral doesn't start at the pyre site, it starts at the home. Once someone has passed away, a family liaison (volunteer) from the End of Life Project, goes to the home and walks the family through everything that is going to happen. The body stays at home for up to three days where family and friends can come and visit. In certain circumstances they would provide a cooling mat that the body would lay on to stay the decomposition process if it was needed.

This is an entirely different experience than the current funeral culture dictates. No funeral home (the staff is able to sign the death certificate), no embalming, just the deceased in their own environment, surrounded by those that love them. It is a fantastic concept and runs back to our natural roots of caring for our dead. This may feel scary or gross to some people but that is only because we have been trained to fear the natural dead body (there are circumstance where this may not be possible). What better way to homage the deceased than to care for them at home, with family. Once

Speaking of the dead by Chelsea L. Tolman

it is time for the cremation, a liaison goes back to the home and assists the family with washing and shrouding the body.

Stephanie led me around to the back of the bamboo fencing, this is where the pallbearers walk with the stretcher to enter. Against the fencing was a shrine-like structure that would hold mementos and pictures of the deceased, not unlike bringing personal belongings and pictures to a mortuary or church. In the center of the space sat the pyre. Some cracks and flaking were present and blackened burn marks covered the interior from previous use. The pyre sat in the center of a circle of sand, reaching about six feet in all directions. The sand was raked into rings encircling the pyre. Enclosing the sand were more stones, hugging the entirety. Then surrounding the stones bare earth, no brush or weeds in danger of catching a spark but benches and chairs for patrons to sit in reverie or mourning or both.

As I am taking all of this in, Stephanie continues the details of what happens here and I continue imagining the process.

Once the body is placed, family and friends are given juniper boughs. This looks like large, fluffy pine tree boughs. The purpose is for tinder for the flame and it gives off a pleasant odor. One by one they place these boughs on top of

223

the body, some people will place notes or other mementos on top to burn with the body as well, similar to what we do in for a traditional funeral of placing things in the casket before burial. There is a Master of Ceremonies, usually a family member or friend, who officiates everything that is to happen. What ceremony takes place here is completely up to the family and how they want to honor their deceased loved one. Once all of these things have taken place, more wood is placed around the body and the fire is lit through small openings on both sides, usually by family members. The flames slowly overtake the body with everyone present. I am told that during this part, everyone is naturally silent, it is a somber, spiritual experience and all watch in reverence as their loved one is engulfed in flame. At some point there reaches a time when there is a release in the air. The tension of getting to this point is over and there is a palpable weight lifted from the crowd. Usually people will start speaking, telling stories or laughing or crying together. What an honor for the deceased and what a relief for the family to be able to experience this incredible journey!

All around the circular fencing are more wooden pillars with decorative handmade clay toppers, some are adorned with crystals (like a wizard's staff) that shine differently at certain angles. On these pillars are copper plaques with the names of those who were cremated and memorialized here, each one is designed by the family and handmade by a local artisan. I can imagine those family members being able to come back to this place and sit on a bench around the pyre, next to their plaque, and remember that day when their loved one was and here set to flame.

I am still in awe that here in the United States, there is a place where a family can care for their loved one in this way. The body isn't taken to a mortuary to be cared for by strangers, the deceased never leaves the family's care. I recognize that this is not a choice that everyone would make and that's okay. After being in the funeral industry for years and caring for bodies for other families and embalming bodies for burial, I am sensitive for the need of different options in funeral rituals and disposition. I also think there is a place in the industry for giving the funeral back to the families who would want that option, maybe not an open-air funeral pyre but the care from time of death to the final disposition, whatever that may be. Laws and regulations are often misinterpreted in the current funeral culture. When I ask if a family wants to have a body embalmed, almost always my question is answered with "Isn't it a law to be embalmed". When I talk to a family about ground burial and the subject of a vault (concrete or metal encasing for the casket) comes up,

225

many people ask, "Well isn't it the law?" No, these things are not laws. There are laws that we must abide by and there are perceived laws for what is really just standard practice, proving that death education is lacking. Family units do not operate the same as in previous years either. Children move away to other parts of the country, cemeteries hold spaces that were bought years previously for family members who have now chosen a different path, meaning the spaces go unused. The majority of people do not think about the end of life until it stares them in the face and sometimes it is just too late and then you just do what everyone else has done only because, that is what has always been done.

WE WILL ALWAYS REMEMBER

The profession of death is much more difficult than most funeral directors make it seem. The public only sees well-dressed professionals, stoic and pressed. We are always there to make everything go just as you planned. However, in the back rooms, grown men and women stand over the body of a teen who has taken their own life and silently wonder, "What could have gone so wrong?" We cradle your dead infants in our arms and revel at their tiny perfections while meticulously wrapping them in clean duck and bunny printed blankets for you to hold them in. We go home after a long day with the smears of mascara on our shoulders from comforting a sobbing, grief-stricken, newly made widows. Our pockets are filled with soggy tissues taken from your hands and whisked out of sight for the sake of decorum. We hold back our emotions when a toddler's are lifted to see their grandmothers lying in a casket and clumsily tuck Crayola colored pictures under grandma's motionless hands, not understanding why nana cannot grasp the treasured paper. The business of death is real, it is raw. We are the kind faced, open armed and seemingly unwrinkled, patient people you see in the lobbies of funeral homes directing you to rooms and standing tall next to a shiny Cadillac hearse. However, the reality is we are people too. We go home and cry over particularly hard cases, we get divorced because spouses can't handle the long hours, and sometimes we break because the stress of this job can be overwhelming.

The day for a funeral director starts just like yours, stumbling out of bed, scrubbing off the sleep and staring back at the image in the mirror with a good ole fashioned pep talk. Yet, we never know what the day ahead has in store for us. We carefully choose our two-piece suit, freshly pressed shirt and sensible shoes that we can get through the day in. Dry cleaning, ironing creases, shining shoes and making sure to have plenty of fresh socks or stockings at the ready is a constant concern in assuring that the families we sit across from and the people attending the funerals see only a well-dressed, put together, professional person who can handle whatever needs to be done, without question. We have perfected the bad hair day dos and eye bag cover-up, without looking like we stuck our faces in cake icing. Rosy cheeks and bright eyes are important in creating the expertly assembled, we can handle it, let us help you and we care type of people that we strive to be for you.

Yet sometimes, we fail at this. Days of little sleep and little time for meals, coupled with an endless stream of dead people and their accompanying screaming, sobbing, shattered family members. The phone hasn't stopped, and the demands pile up, along with heaps of paperwork. We explain the difference between laws and rules and how they govern the ways bodies can be handled. We make phone calls pleading to the cemetery or florist or airline to do just this one favor so that a family can create the final farewell they had envisioned for a newly dead person who was a mother, grandfather, son or spouse.

Upstairs change into a suit, downstairs change into embalming gear. To the cemetery. To the vital records office. Sitting on the phone arranging the details of a funeral while waiting in the lobby of a church between other funerals. Filling out paperwork, gently guiding the grieving through the overwhelming of choices available. Feeling like maybe even with all of the choices available, nothing is exactly what the family needed. We are in constant motion.

Then, life at home. A spouse, children, a sick parent, friends and neighbors, laundry, house cleaning, soccer games, choir practice, doctor's appointments, the dog died, the yard needs mowing, the furnace stopped working. These things are real too and need the same attention and care and love and

Speaking of the dead by Chelsea L. Tolman

patience a profession dealing with human emotion and grief. All of this is done while being paid a pittance for the effort and being granted insufficient time off to attend to these matters, let alone respite for our own tired and weary bones. So, sometimes the tender, patient and soft part of a human, under these conditions of pushing, pulling and being taxed beyond its limits fails.

I remember them, the faces of families that I have served. I remember when I wasn't enough, when I knew I wasn't present enough, at work or at home. I remember the waves of doubt and guilt that I could handle things as I was pushed to the edge of my ability. I remember their slightly down-turned eyes as I tried to urge myself through a really hard day and ended up bringing uncertainty to those who needed me to be certain. The tear-filled but silent judgments of those who needed strength but at that moment, I was just as broken as the person I was supposed to be shouldering.

Not everyone will understand or give leeway when things go wrong. Even on the best of days things are missed, misinterpreted, or forgotten for any number of reasons. Human error, a buried email, lack of follow up or details forgotten. Sometimes it's okay, but in every circumstance

Speaking of the dead by Chelsea L. Tolman

where it was okay, a funeral director remembers. We let it sink in over and over, and through all of the strain and pull of everything we strive to be and sometimes cannot, I promise you that when something breaks down or isn't delivered or goes horribly wrong, it is not on purpose or for the lack of caring or trying. Failure isn't an option in this business, so when it happens, we will always remember.

Speaking of the dead by Chelsea L. Tolman

You can find out more about Chelsea by visiting her website www.ChelseaTolman.com and of course you can follow her on all the favorite media channels Facebook, Instagram and Twitter.

Made in the USA
Middletown, DE
16 November 2018